THE POWER OF FREEDOM

DENIS LETENDRE

IUNIVERSE, INC.
BLOOMINGTON

The Power of Freedom

iUniverse books may be ordered through booksellers or by contacting:

iUniverse
1663 Liberty Drive
Bloomington, IN 47403
www.iuniverse.com
1-800-Authors (1-800-288-4677)

Because of the dynamic nature of the Internet, any web addresses or links contained in this book may have changed since publication and may no longer be valid.

ISBN: 978-1-4502-7658-0 (sc)
ISBN: 978-1-4502-7660-3 (dj)
ISBN: 978-1-4502-7659-7 (ebk)

Printed in the United States of America

iUniverse rev. date: 12/30/2010

To my patient wife Sandy, for standing by me through a lot of challenges. To my children, Christiane and Daniel and a special young lady, Bianca Rose who give me hope for the future.

Contents

PREFACE

In a world that is losing its meaning of freedom, let me offer you a counter-idea and a way back to real liberty. Freedom, as it was defined by the French and American revolutions, has evolved in the last two hundred years. Lawyers have been redefining its meaning to something quite different from the founding fathers' interpretation.

My name is Denis Letendre; I am a baby boomer and ex-hippie. I conducted a social experiment thirty-five years ago and stumbled across an energy and power that I feel needs to be revealed now. This energy needs to be released now more than ever if mankind is going to face its challenges, solve its problems, and survive. As Albert Einstein said, "The significant problems we face cannot be solved at the same level of thinking we were at when we created them." A real change—a change from within—is the only lasting solution. All of us experiment with drugs or other substances until we find what works for us; however, my experiment with substance use has given me a unique perspective on freedom. In a world that misunderstands freedom, I must shout aloud its true meaning and potential!

INTRODUCTION

Where do I begin? How would you begin to explain a discovery that you believe is so important that you are compelled to write? I was born in 1950. I guess that makes me a baby boomer. The significance of my generation can be found in our sheer number, for starters, and then what comes to mind is Vietnam, the Kennedys, the moon landing, and the emergence of computers and various new technologies.

It was a time of stay-at-home moms, big cars, and a whole lot of mindsets. The mindsets of the WWII generation came directly into conflict with ours. The emergence of the hippie phenomenon and the introduction of lots of new and fun drugs created almost another religion of peace and love. This hippie culture was a bizarre development, when you think about it! It really rocked the establishment with its hairstyles and free love. I remember it well: as soon as I reached the age of reason, I started questioning established norms of behavior. It is the timeless question: *Why?* Why is this the way it is? Why is this the acceptable way to live?

I have to stand back here a little because you know as well as I that probably every new generation since the beginning of time has asked the same question. It must be the nature of what could be called progress. You have to ask yourself, "If I negate a past foolish behavior but do not replace it with an improvement, is that progress?" It is always very easy to be the critic—saying no, no, no to everything and never really saying yes to anything, because that might be considered a commitment, and you could be wrong.

My goal in the following pages is to communicate how and where my discovery of an enormous source of energy took place. This energy had been hiding in plain sight through the centuries, and I wonder why no one had ever noticed it. Why me?

I asked the same questions as the members of many other new generations before mine, but I experimented in making alternative choices in behavior. This experiment is what you will be reading about in the following pages. The solutions to all the world's current problems already exist in minds not yet awakened to alternate possibilities. You may find me a little annoying as I try to describe changes in thinking and attitudes toward perceived realities, but bear with me.

So what's up with the title *Power of Freedom*? The "power" in what you will read is not to be confused with a forced ideology, like the type of thinking behind the relocation of Native Americans on reservations. The word "power" in this context means *energy*. The United States has always been known as the land of opportunity, where freedom and the Bill of Rights gives everyone the chance to pursue his or her dreams. Even though the power to pursue our dreams has created the most prosperous society in history, that power is *not* what I discovered.

As you read these pages, my hope is that you'll understand that I am not discussing morally right or wrong behavior or an affiliation with any religion or political belief. The observations discussed here are from my own personal experiences over forty years.

Please be clear that any references to drugs and substances include alcohol and nicotine. Let's not kid ourselves!

I am excited at the state of our society at this time in history. We are poised for great change to take place. Change will happen regardless, but the course of that change will depend on the decisions we make in this land of the free.

CHAPTER 1

THE FIVE-YEAR EXPERIMENT

To document the series of events that led to my interpretation of freedom, I need to share with you a significant time in my life. Let's go back forty years to when I was seventeen and preparing for graduation. During high school, I was extremely straight. I was into bodybuilding and wrestling and didn't take drugs or drink alcohol. I had no intention of going to college, because I felt that no career was worth my full investment. My one burning desire was freedom—the freedom to express myself. I was attracted to the rebellious attitude of the Beatles' look and music. While every generation rebels to some degree, my interest in the Beatles was more of a fashion statement than a rebellion. My parents strongly disapproved and made my life miserable.

THE EXPERIMENT BEGINS

Graduation time was exciting, because my goal was to get out of school. After graduation came party time and my introduction to alcohol. Drinking was an experiment. I discovered that alcohol made me feel good, but it also made me feel sick. In either case, it was fun. I worked for my dad and had other jobs as well. I was responsible at work but enjoyed partying afterward. I was trying to develop my self-image by imitating the looks and actions of cool people like the Beatles.

It is amazing how alcohol mixed with my attitude to change my self-image and personality. Having fun and feeling good was the background to my belief that my actions and lifestyle represented who I was. I was already fabricating an illusion of myself, and I was buying into it 100 percent. I was making myself into something I was not and believing it. It is amazing how humans can rationalize their behavior because of feelings.

I do not want to portray some kind of "right or wrong" or "good or evil" scenario, but I had certainly discovered an example of an activity that affects the thinking mind. Alcohol loosens inhibitions. Under the influence of alcohol, the human mind is less aware of the natural tension between opposing forces like yin and yang. That lessening tension is the direct result of the mind *not thinking*. When we don't think, we base decisions on emotions.

The cycle repeated itself every time I tried to relieve the tension through alcohol. Relieving the tension was fun! Feeling good was an easier way to live than thinking logically, but I was deceiving myself. I was trying to make myself into the person I pictured in my mind, and drinking alcohol helped to create that new me. Of course, I had no idea that I was beginning the process of altering my perception of reality.

I viewed alcohol as a drug with a certain effect, and I looked for other drugs that might have a different effect, such as marijuana. Within three months of graduating from high school, I had my first experiences with marijuana and LSD, along with the resulting emotional highs and lows. It was fun! Relationships with females were purely for fun, pleasure, and sex. It was easy when using drugs or alcohol. I could manipulate my feelings to whatever seemed cool.

EMOTIONAL DECISIONS EQUAL EMOTIONAL RESULTS

This lifestyle lasted about five years. I tried different combinations of drugs and alcohol. Using these substances changed my perception of reality. For example, when I used the mind-altering drug LSD and got high during a church service, religion seemed absurd. It didn't make sense.

The whole hippie thing basically turned all accepted social morals upside down. Even while I was in the middle of this hippie culture, I was still observing what was happening all around me, though my perspective was tainted. I was immersed in having a good time, using whatever substance would enhance my lifestyle, but at the same time, I was studying the behavior of all kinds of people around me who were also using drugs. A female walking around half naked and high seemed a little odd, but I wasn't about to complain; I was part of the situation.

I thought a new culture was developing out of the new drugs and the feelings about the Vietnam War. Accepted norms of moral and social order were breaking down. I loved it! It seemed like something to believe in. At the same time, I wondered about the long-term effects on America and other free societies. Replacing a lot of traditions and socially accepted behavior with the liberty of free choice should justify itself and lead society to a better place, I reasoned.

People who didn't embrace this new freedom were classified as being "straight." Such people didn't question anything; for the most part, they pursued careers and goals in traditional ways. In one sense, this created two classes of people: the freedom seekers, who ignored all restrictions, and the straight people who held tightly to conservative social norms. Though totally immersed in the freedom lifestyle, I could still see that both opinions had merit.

I was never so detached from reality that I didn't understand the need for money to finance this newly found free lifestyle. So naturally, I worked steadily for the most money I could make. Alcohol and drugs weren't cheap! But I was cool! I prided myself that I could hide from anyone what was really going on inside me, I could work and do sports; I could meet girls and straight people, and they wouldn't know about my other lifestyle. I was playing a game.

It is difficult to be objective with this type of attitude. Make no mistake about it: I was truly buying into my newly found lifestyle; more importantly, I was totally convinced that I was turning into the real me. I was doing my thing, which was who I was. No human could have convinced me otherwise!

Accepting any and all lifestyles was part of this new freedom generation. However the cards fell—if someone got addicted or changed sexual preference, for example—that was all cool. From this perspective, marriage was unnecessary. Who cared if two people wanted to live together? With free-spirited thinking running on its own gas, there is no end to the imaginative alternative lifestyles that can come into existence. At the time, I thought, *So what? Whatever makes people happy!* Even the great United States Constitution states that people have the freedom to pursue happiness.

Naturally, the differing interpretations of freedom by free-spirited people and straights led to major misunderstandings. So there I was, in the seventies, heading toward the foreseeable future, the twenty-first century. I was constantly working on myself, trying to find the coolest combination or single substance to truly be the real me. It was fun, I must admit, since the refusal to stand on any principles required no commitment! After all, commitment would infringe on my sense of freedom. I could commit to having a job, though, for the steady income to pay for the substances I was choosing freely.

IRONIES OF SUBSTANCE USE

Let me relate the effect that various substances had on my life by discussing two of the most dangerous, yet most socially acceptable, substances in society: alcohol and cigarettes. Despite their dangers, both are legal in most parts of the world. Alcohol, especially, is widely accepted and considered nonthreatening to society when consumed in an acceptable way. Our culture has an unwritten law of when and how to consume alcohol that seems strange, at the very least.

To the inexperienced person, the first drink or cigarette is repulsive. Hangovers and coughing should send a negative message to a person. Yet these substances remain legal. To me, consuming these substances was fun, because it loosened inhibitions and made me feel good. If I overdid it, I would get sick and get a hangover. In a weird way, even a hangover was cool and acceptable to society, making it very easy to continue the process.

Alcohol differed from other drugs in one major effect: it didn't alter reality in the same way. Consider the Woodstock Festival in New York in August 1969. The participants weren't passing around whiskey and beer. People were high for days, but they were not drunk. Free love and peace seemed to be by-products of the hallucinogens. It was a great time, but part of me looked at this event from a detached perspective. These people were the next generation; in the face of real issues, they were tearing down old concepts, but they didn't offer any new concepts with which to deal with those issues. What would the future bring?

Although I wondered about these ideas, I was basically indifferent, because I was happy and having a good time. For an intense period of five years, I indulged in all the substances, except heroin and crack; they were not cool because of their extremely addictive properties. Finding the right combination of substances to fit my mood or personality wasn't easy. Using substances to create the real me probably came from wanting significance in my life. I wanted to be somebody!

It was an ego thing. My dad offered me $2,000 to stop using marijuana and other substances. Given my strong sense of freedom, no amount of money could have changed my behavior, because I firmly believed that my choices defined who I was. I was part of a large segment of society who weren't really suited to chasing a career to find success. But I observed that even career-oriented people were engaged in substance use.

The combination of working to afford a lifestyle and partying was creating a personality that was slowly becoming me. I could juggle various substances to create the effects I wanted. I could get along with anyone, because I accepted everybody's lifestyle.

Hippie drugs were the most sexually liberating. Alcohol may have lessened inhibitions, but it also made me pass out. Drugs, when used properly, made it seem natural to satisfy my sexual urges. The early hippie era spoke of love and peace, which are easy words to say and feel when you are high. Being stoned seemed all natural and the way humans should live. Amazingly, some people made a kind of religion out of it. There were some who theorized that it was the "alkies" (short for straight people who drank alcohol) who were responsible for Vietnam, segregation, and all the other problems in society. This sentiment grew strongest in the sixties. The seventies brought forth the yuppie transition. Without the Vietnam War, all that idealism and laying of blame on conservative straights seemed unnecessary.

TODAY'S VERSION OF THE EXPERIMENT

During the decades since my experiment, the pervasive substance use has continued. In addition to alcohol, cocaine became popular, and with it came a fresh wave of party-positive attitude. The free-spirited people from the sixties had not replaced the old ideology with a new system of values. Perhaps they had thought that freedom would be a natural progression, an idea worth holding on to and a philosophy all by itself. When freedom of expression became more acceptable, freedom took on a new meaning, as expressed in the popular Isley Brothers song, *It's Your Thing.*

This transition is very important, because the perceived power of freedom arose from the individual's ability to choose any lifestyle that made him or her happy. From my perspective at the time, this was where society should be going. Civilization was advancing and becoming more sophisticated, and a lot of change seemed to be coordinated with the increase and diversity of substance use. The United States Constitution seems to back up this ideology.

All that I have been relating of these five years of substance use, including my observations about society, would have been just very common and typical of most adolescents if a change in events had not occurred.

Between 1968 and 1973, I learned I liked alcohol and drugs. I knew the effects and felt totally in control. It was fun, and I knew what made me feel good. I had friends, a steady job, and a sportive life.

WHY CHANGE?

So why did I change? Why did I decide to stop using mind-altering substances? Using substances gave me the illusion of understanding the mysteries of the universe. Why did I walk away from that increased sense of awareness and the pleasure of doing anything I wanted to do?

For reasons still unknown to me, one night as I was going to sleep, I became aware that the experiment was no longer objective, because my perceptions had been altered. I responded emotionally and cried. That was when I decided to alter my choices of behavior based on logic, not emotion, and see what happens.

The freedom of choice to engage in a lifestyle of substance use and the observations I made during those five years had produced some very revealing and difficult conclusions.

1. All drugs had an effect; they were fun and made me feel good.
2. They all changed my perception of reality.
3. With enough effort, I could get addicted to any one of them.

4. Continued use of drugs to change my mood or personality could have changed my sexual orientation.

5. Substance use changed my belief structure.

What I am today as a result of drug use is so different to the very core from who I was before my experiment that it amazes me. I am a product of the sixties, of the Vietnam War, of hippies. My generation began to realize that changes needed to take place, and "do your own thing" became a slogan. But freedom and change don't always solve all the problems. Sometimes they create their own problems.

The drugs, especially marijuana and LSD, made everything beautiful and colorful, with an emphasis on love and peace. But these drugs also had a unique ability to make the ideas and rules of society seem absurd. Organized religion, sexual restrictions, marriage, war—everything looked ridiculous when viewed through the drugs. All that mattered was freedom and pleasure.

MY AWAKENING TO A REDEFINING OF FREEDOM

The sixties' concept of freedom valued change simply for the sake of change, not for the purpose of replacing the old ideas with something better. Freedom was glorified as a stand-alone right, self-justified. There is no power in freedom standing on its own. Freedom is only a gateway to power, not power in itself. Becoming aware of the changes occurring in the sixties and the absurdity of the direction society was going amazed me. Here is an example: I tried different drugs in an effort to find the best combination that would help me become who I wanted to be. I reasoned that marijuana is better than alcohol because it is natural, right? I tried to make intelligent choices about which substances were best for me; I rationalized my decisions.

But rationalization didn't work for long. I suddenly became aware that ingesting any drug was illogical. I had to separate myself from my feelings and recognize the truth that ingesting, drinking, or smoking whatever drug served no purpose other than a few hours of feel-good fun. Once I started this wave of reasoning, my whole universe of perception began to change.

I had freely engaged in substance use during the experiment; now I was going to use that same freedom to make radical alternative choices. It was not a question of good or bad. I am not saying that drinking or doing drugs is a good thing or a bad thing. I am not going to play some kind of moral judge. In redefining my understanding of freedom, I discovered an immense energy capable of both physically and mentally changing the human condition. That is the purpose of this book, not to scold or judge. Stay on patiently while I explain the origins of that energy.

CHAPTER 2

EXPLORING THE ILLOGICAL

What I find amazing is how my perspective changed when I chose to stop using substances. In studying my own human condition, I found a road map guided by my individual impulses, cravings, and feelings that provided the energy for change from within. Change began with choices made from a base of freedom. That sense of freedom has been growing within, and it affects my perception of the world.

Since I am aware of an internal road map, I have to assume that all humans have it. I am different from and yet the same as anyone else. Governments, religion, gangs, and social environments should never be given the power to control each individual's internal road map. It is the key to humankind's ability to find happiness and fulfillment, not to mention solutions to our challenges as a species on this planet.

My compassion for humans beings increased as time passed. I saw others as no different than I, except in the way they chose to exercise their perceived freedom.

Why do people choose illogical behavior? Let's explore the world of illogical choices.

EXAMPLES OF ILLOGICAL BEHAVIOR

First let's consider two examples of physical needs common to all human beings: food and sex.

Food is essential for physical human life, but consuming more food than is necessary for nutrition is illogical. Yet every day, people eat far more food than they need. Why? They like the taste of food; they enjoy the pleasure of eating. They don't realize that food is a substance that can be abused; overeating can become an addiction.

Sex can also become an addiction. The purpose of sexual intercourse is procreation, but because the human sex drive is strong and because sexual intercourse or masturbation produces pleasure, people indulge in sex outside of marriage or through pornography in an attempt to satisfy their sexual urges. Such activity is illogical.

Food and sexual satisfaction are recurring needs that cannot be satisfied permanently. But by thinking logically and considering purpose instead of pleasure only, we can realize greater satisfaction from nutrition and sex over a lifetime.

When I began to turn away from using substances for pleasure, I viewed women from a new perspective. I saw them as different, but equal—and deserving of the greatest respect.

Unfortunately, most people make choices based on short-term satisfaction or pleasure rather than logic. They rationalize overeating, for example, by saying that food is necessary for survival, but they don't think about the amount of food they need.

Thinking is often a tedious or painful process. It is easier to lie to ourselves than to think logically. Thomas Edison said that most people would rather die than think. Why? Do they fear a thinking overdose? Are they afraid of going mental? Do they suffer a fear of the unknown? These are baseless fears. Over the years, I've come to embrace the strange feelings in my head that occur when I am thinking. I haven't gone crazy. On the contrary, I have developed an overall sense of well-being.

Consider other examples. Does a person who is about to sexually abuse another ask himself or herself, *What am I doing? Why am I doing this?* Of course not! Long before abuse begins, the person should have learned to recognize and choose logical behavior over illogical behavior. Consider drunkenness. Is it conceivable that in an advanced civilization, thinking people would sit in a bar and get drunk? Is that logical?

Addiction to anything—food, sex, alcohol, other drugs, pornography, anything—neutralizes the power that comes from the true freedom of thinking and choosing logically. Any person, anywhere on the planet, no matter the country, can use logic to tap into the power of freedom. The solutions that the planet needs will require participation from all people. Their diversity will contribute to a unique change in the perception of reality that develops uniquely in each person.

My own metamorphosis was pretty simple, compared to the potential of other people. I turned to books for more knowledge and changed my perception of sex, but other people will have different experiences, depending on their orientations. My purpose is becoming more and more evident as time goes on, just as other people will discover their unique paths.

True freedom comes from within, but there is a price to be paid. How is it possible to give people their freedom and expect them to value it? It is not. They must choose freedom. They must choose to think! If fear of the unknown is what keeps masses of people from thinking, they must realize that the answers to all questions are to be found in the great unknown.

I had thought that getting high was the path to more freedom, but that was an illusion. Simply deciding freely not to consume these substances changed everything! From my perspective today, it seems that people who choose to consume these substances rationalize their behavior to avoid thinking and to create an alternative reality. They convince themselves that getting high is freedom and that illogical behavior is logical.

THE BENEFIT OF LOGIC

At its best, logical behavior is unselfish. It benefits not only the individual but others as well. For example, all humans have a built-in desire to stay alive, but when a person chooses to kill another person, the very act jeopardizes his own existence! Thus, he will avoid such violence, respecting others in order to indirectly further his own chances of survival. In order for humans to coexist peacefully, people must be able to trust each other. When one person acts deceitfully, he sows distrust and corrupts society. Such behavior is illogical, because it damages both the individual and the community in general.

Accessing the power of freedom can open the door to solving problems within society. What is this power? It is the energy created when two opposing forces coexist in harmony. When you clap your two hands together and rub them against one another, the friction produces heat; that's energy. Connecting to the two poles of a car battery produces a spark of heat; that's energy. The coming together of two opposites seems to be the common denominator.

So when the mind is given two options, one at odds with emotion and one at odds with logic, the resulting tension is energy; it intensifies the thinking process. Because we perceive that tension as uncomfortable, we discard it as undesirable. Unfortunately, that response has kept the masses from realizing another level of thinking potential.

Take a simple example. Suppose a person has developed the habit of using vulgar language. He discovers that his language often offends people and causes relationships to deteriorate. Because he has the freedom to choose his language, he can decide to stop and replace his expletives with less offensive language. But habit is a powerful thing. So when he is talking to someone, and he has to decide whether to use vulgarity, he will feel a momentary tension, which is normal.

Thinking first and *then* deciding to use the less offensive word to communicate without harming a relationship creates energy. That energy physically affects the brain's thinking process and also the body. Sounds pretty simple, right? Isn't it logical to choose words that improve relationships rather than damage them?

When a choice is made from logic, weird feelings or tensions surface. These sensations are not bad; they indicate a source of energy trying to make itself known. You have to let the energy do its thing. It will affect your mind and thinking. It is not easy, but anyone can engage in it.

Here's another example. You are with other people who are drinking alcohol, but you choose not to consume it. You will feel uncomfortable; you will ask yourself, *Why am I doing this?* Keep to your decision; do not be afraid. Let the energy or feeling do its thing. It will take time. Days, weeks, and months will pass, but eventually you will notice all kinds of changes in your perception and awareness.

We associate the thinking process with the classroom, but the vast majority of human genius is released independent of academia. Every human being has a path or a purpose to his or her existence that can only be discovered in an environment of freedom.

Freedom is only the doorway, not the key. The key is activating the mind through thinking to create enormous energy, which develops change from within. The more a society relinquishes its thinking to religion, government, or emotion, the smaller the pool of humans available to find solutions for the planet's challenges. We need the whole planet, with all of its cultures and its diverse historical background, to think logically. Everyone can tap into this tremendous source of energy to start the metamorphosis from within.

FINDING THE FREEDOM

Today's society, with its modern interpretation of freedom, has rationalized various knee-jerk or escapist responses to unpleasant feelings or tensions, so that no energy is produced. Let me give you an example. A child has a thorn stuck in his leg. He would be screaming for you to make it feel good, but he doesn't want you to touch the thorn or remove it, so he hides the wound, even though the unpleasant feeling of removing the thorn and the subsequent pain of healing is necessary to make the leg better.

As previously stated, all choices must be made free of government, religion, family, and social influences. This doesn't mean that these institutions are not vitally important. Government, for instance (assuming it does not transgress the rights of the individual), is very important in a civilized society. Government best serves the common interests of all people in areas like transportation, education, and security. Government exists for the people, not the people for the government. To be effective, government needs people who fully engage their minds in thinking based on free will and who strive for the highest ideals in their personal lives.

Religion also serves a vital role in society. No religion should take away the freedom of choice. Whatever religion one chooses should support the highest pursuits of the individual, and if it does not, the individual should find a religion that is totally in harmony with that pursuit.

The family is the nucleus of society and is vital in the healthy growth of its members. Even though our choices need to be free of family influences, until a child has reached the age of reason, of course the parents need to make the choices. That age of reason is different for each child. The development of children to adulthood absolutely needs the influence of strong parental leadership. Without that leadership, the nonsense and confusion of puberty sometimes leads to rebellion, with no progress toward the pursuit of excellence.

Prior to the sixties revolution, I had plenty of religious and family pressures. The alcohol and the hippie drugs that were popular at the time affected how I perceived and related to religion and family. I studied how different substances affected my attitude. For a while, alcohol was cool, and then only drugs like marijuana and LSD were cooler than just wine. Around and around I would go, rationalizing that every feel-good, mood-altering drug could make me who I was. Amazing!

What makes my experience so unusual is that I stood at the very edge of so many different addicting lifestyles, believing that each was truly who I was. Then I made a choice free of any addiction: to think! That decision and choice has catapulted my existence to something light-years beyond anything I thought possible. I have barely begun, and the future is extremely exciting.

THE NEED FOR TRUE FREEDOM

Our government cannot find solutions to our many challenges until "We the People" who created the government in the first place begin a change from within. We cannot release the power of freedom without first stopping our knee-jerk reaction to the tensions we face every day in our personal choices when emotion and logic conflict. I don't expect the majority of the people to be disrupted from their complacent lives by these mere words, but I know that some eyes will be opened—enough to begin a chain reaction similar to that surrounding a stone thrown into a still pond. The ripples extend throughout the pond.

When the United States Constitution was being drafted, the authors were trying to form a more perfect union. They were trying to remove the flaws from the known forms of government that existed in their time. Are we today trying to perfect our government by simply expanding our definition of freedom to encompass the ridiculous? Compounding one illogical thought process with another doesn't produce a logical result! We cannot solve our problems today unless we remove the thorn and treat the wound.

You see, my words strike at the very core of the human condition, which has in essence contributed to all of today's challenges. If we can rationalize the destruction of human life shortly after its conception because of stress, inconvenience, or bad feelings, how much different and inconvenient and stressful will life be when humans are living longer in nursing homes? Does it take much imagination to rationalize euthanasia into a supposedly logical process toward creating a more perfect union? Life is inconvenient at the beginning and at the end of its existence.

During the five-year experiment, abortion was a nonissue, because it was simple. We are free to feel good; if a pregnancy doesn't feel good, then terminate it—not complicated.

This is not a judgment on my part, just an observation. There are so many examples in our society, and this one seemed easy enough.

Terminating human life is considered murder and illegal. Preservation of life is logical. Issues like abortion and euthanasia clearly show how emotions are used to rationalize illogical behavior. Whatever feels good wins! As a result, no energy is created. The energy that could have been created from the two opposite poles of emotion and logic is not allowed to evolve to a higher level of thinking. In addition, we add the standard of legality or illegality to the mix of emotional choices. Passing a law to make abortion legal does not make it logical.

Our evolution as a species does not depend on what form of government we have or what laws we pass but rather on the level of thinking we pursue. Our thinking is what creates our government and laws. If we as a nation are pursuing a more perfect union, what standard are we aiming at? If our standard of freedom is defined as "whatever makes us feel good," the rest of the world should fear us as a potential threat to their security. If "We the People" created the government, we cannot expect the government to solve our problems until "We the People" change our thinking from within.

Though I have changed my behavior from the feel-good, five-year experiment, I have not left behind the emotional stimuli that I had back then. To this day, I still experience the stress and tension in each choice I make, but the difference is that I recognize the energy at work and allow it to continue so that my thinking evolves to a higher level. This symbiosis between emotion and logic leaves no room for boredom. Boredom is a very dangerous state of consciousness that I hope never to accept.

Unless our nation has a vision of what a more perfect union is, how can we attain it? Even when reaching for the unattainable star, we are still guided toward its light. Feeling good and being at peace with oneself are two distinctly different states of being. Feeling good indicates a temporary but immediate satisfaction of an emotional desire. Peace is a state of being encompassing the total human, comprising both emotion and intellect. It accepts logical rather than emotional satisfaction.

If we, as a nation, believe that everyone should feel good about whatever behavior he or she chooses, we will spend all our time legalizing every possible feel-good experience in a vain effort to make everyone happy. That kind of happiness—or freedom, as some interpret it—is an illusion.

Consider the attitude we have in our society about self-esteem. We constantly hear about the need to nurture, protect, and develop self-esteem among children and adults. Apparently, we create self-esteem in people by praising them and rewarding them even when they fail.

You have to be kidding me! Parents may be able to develop an environment where self-esteem can grow, but self-esteem can only be earned and realized by the individual person. Gratifying every feel-good emotional urge doesn't produce an environment for developing self-esteem. Striving for excellence, recognizing weaknesses, and overcoming obstacles helps an individual develop self-esteem. No one can give another person self-esteem.

Our society today is trying to dethrone religion and moral codes in the name of freedom. Yes, it is reasonable to review institutions and moral codes, but to utterly discard them is absurd and destructive to society, unless the proposed conceptual replacement is an improvement. Today, many people are trying to legalize emotional, feel-good, personal decisions. But imposing personal choices on society as a whole does not make those choices logical or productive. If we are striving for a more perfect union, we must make laws based on logic, not emotion.

When I was under the influence of hallucinogenic substances, organized religion seemed very absurd. Does that mean it really is absurd? No. Could there be a connection between the baby-boomer generation and the subsequent development of a malaise about organized religion as a whole? Maybe we have created an illusion of a threat to our freedom with our limited understanding of the role of religion in our society! No religion should threaten our freedom of choice. When religion does cross the line, it is called a cult. That happens when a religious organization manipulates people through a type of brainwashing to remove the awareness of freedom of choice.

As we pursue a more perfect union, it is easy to see the effects of society's failure to form a higher standard. Just look at headlines and news stories from recent months: failing corporations ripping off the system with US bailouts, more babies being born out of wedlock than ever, the nation borrowing trillions of dollars to pay debt, and cultural clashes about same-sex marriages, to mention only a few. Our laws cannot regulate our behavior on a personal level. The real power of freedom has yet to be released in our society.

BUT HOW?

How can the real power of freedom become an active force in our society? The answer is simple: start thinking! Anyone can begin the process now. Because of the unique differences among us—age, sex, and cultural background, to name a few—I will keep it as simple as possible. Let's start where you are right now. Remember, if you are addicted to a behavior or the consumption of a substance, that behavior has to be stopped, and your thinking and attitude about this changed behavior must be seen from a new perspective in order to derive any sense of power from the initiative.

All choices must be made freely in order to generate any power. Let us start with little steps. Stop consuming any substances that produce a temporary, feel-good response (drugs, alcohol, nicotine). These are obviously illogical options. That will get the ball rolling.

Too hard or too radical? Start a little at a time until the behavior is terminated. Depending on your pre-existing habits of consumption, this adjustment may start generating energy very quickly. At first and for quite a while, depending on the person, the feeling will be more a tension and frustration than a sense of energy. Hang in there until you start to notice the energy.

Don't play rationalization games with yourself. Don't say, "I'll have a drink because it's my birthday or New Year's Eve." Come on; get real. I have gotten married twice and did not toast with alcohol at either celebration. Nor did I indulge in any substances when I got divorced. Drinking was illogical behavior at either end of the spectrum. Think instead, and the energy that produces will grow stronger as time goes by. Build each logical choice on the previous one.

This first step of eliminating substance consumption is a big one for obvious reasons. It strikes very deep at the heart of our culture and lifestyle, as such substances are too often confused with the pursuit of happiness and *joie de vivre*. Changing behavior in just this one area will start a whole change in the wiring of your thinking patterns. You cannot escape the shift in perspective, so hold on for the ride. It will not be boring! This change in behavior will get the energy rolling quickly.

If this is too much for you, start with something less physically challenging than substance use. You may indulge in other activities that are just as illogical. Earlier I mentioned the habit of using vulgar language. Be aware of and terminate vulgar language before it comes out. It is an illogical form of communication. Again, be real! Don't rationalize that vulgar language is the only way to communicate effectively. Start small, and you will feel the energy at work. You will engage your thinking in a way you never realized possible.

Lying is also illogical. You may say this is crazy, but letting go of illogical behavior opens the door to the real power of freedom! Think about it. You were probably taught that lying is wrong, so you feel guilty when you tell a lie. People rationalize all kinds of behavior in order to feel comfortable with behavior that initially gave them a sense of guilt. Humans cannot live peacefully with themselves with constant guilt, so they deaden guilt with rationalization. They lie to themselves and eventually believe the lie. Now that is weird!

A FEW MORE WORDS ABOUT SEX

One of the major forces in society is our attitude toward sex. Our modern society has commercialized sex and distorted its real purpose to a bizarre extent. Our sexual lives are another very powerful means of opening the door to massive energy and the true power of freedom. Altering our sexual behavior will set off a whole series of changes that will quickly change our entire perspective about sex.

I can hear the controversy already heating up. Today's society has put such a positive spin on sex that it is classified right up there with the four major food groups of healthy living. We have rationalized every kind of behavior in this area in order to remove any guilt people have. Even the so-called learned psychologists have gotten into it.

Are you ready for the single most influential activity change you can make in order to create tremendous energy, open the door to the power of freedom, and immediately start rewiring your thinking pattern? Stop masturbating! Many people of both sexes practice this activity as a right of puberty, yet it is blatantly illogical. It serves no purpose other than pleasure. The whole physiological process of sexual stimulation is a prelude to intercourse for the procreation of our species, not some alternate natural form of pleasure inducement.

Today's interpretation of freedom as including our right to use our bodies any way we see fit has led to rationalization of all kinds of illogical sexual activity. We justify pornography as freedom of expression and same-sex marriage as a constitutional right. How do these activities relate to masturbation? The practice of masturbating increases the need to find satisfaction. The temporary satisfaction is just that—temporary. When a person establishes sexual gratification by any means available as a need that we cannot do without, we leap to the conclusion that this need has to be protected by our constitution. The spin our modern society has given to the whole subject is really noteworthy.

The fact of the matter is, no matter how strong the sexual urges are, failure to satisfy them will not harm you. But if a human engages in enough of this self-induced sexual pleasure, the activity will become an addictive behavior. As with all other guilt-inducing behavior, we will then find a way to rationalize this continuing behavior.

When two members of the opposite sex or same sex feel an attraction, at that moment of awareness, a decision must be made as to whether to pursue the relationship. Same-sex sexual activity is not logical, because procreation cannot take place. Opposite-sex activity is logical, but physical intimacy must be delayed until a long-term commitment can be established to the best of the couple's ability.

Why, you may ask? In the event that a baby appears on the scene, the mother and father must share in its survival and mental development and well-being. Procreation is one of the highest purposes of our existence and cannot be treated lightly. Our modern society today has devised all sorts of rationalized viewpoints on the subject. Our scientists have discovered new ways of birth control to make it easy to circumvent the baby-making aspect of intercourse, but to what purpose?

Just think for a moment of all the industries and products that derive from masturbation. Pornography exists to feed our pleasure game. If masturbation were terminated, a person would not want to further antagonize the sexual arousal with pornography. That's the end of the massive pornography issue as we know it. *Think!* When I stopped masturbating, I didn't want to aggravate the situation with pornography. Why would I want to become aroused when I had decided that this type of gratification is illogical?

More importantly, soon after I stopped that behavior, my perception of sex changed. The way I looked at women changed completely, and any relation with them changed to something special. I no longer looked at them as a means of pleasuring myself. I could respect their freedom as well as my own.

FREEDOM OF CHOICE IS FOR EVERYONE

Freedom of choice is a right of all people. Respecting that right to freedom of choice without coercion gives society as a whole liberty. That basic liberty is the foundation from which to access the power of freedom. For example, when I started changing my behavior, I felt a strong urge to impose my ideas on other people. That would have been a violation of another's right to free choice without intimidation

Our society today has formulated opinions and so-called intelligent scientific data rationalizing our ludicrous behavior just to neutralize the guilt our behavior initially creates. I say initially because in time, our own minds weave patterns of acceptance of our illogical behavior. As mentioned earlier, a human cannot live in peace with illogical behavior without first removing the guilt. Today, we have effectively neutralized the credibility of religion, government, and authority of any kind when it comes to determining what behavior is acceptable in our free society.

I stand as a living testimony to the fact that a doorway to the real power of freedom exists. Great energy can transport the human intellect to a much higher plane of existence. As the transformation takes place, our perception of reality changes.

With that changed perception will come solutions to all of the world's challenges.

ASKING THE RIGHT QUESTION

To start the thinking process, we must ask the most important question: *Why?* Mankind has been asking this question throughout recorded history. This question becomes personal when it is applied to the individual who is willing to ask himself, *Why am I taking this action?* For example, to a smoker who chooses not to smoke, that choice becomes very personal, especially if addiction has set in. With every moment that goes by, the question becomes more intense: *Why did I stop smoking?* The answer is simple: *I stopped smoking because it is an illogical, unproductive behavior.* But until the smoker gets comfortable with that answer, the immediate struggle will continue.

Given enough time, enough days of choosing not to smoke, the smoker will get to the other side of the answer. The resulting energy will become more important and more useful than the illogical behavior of smoking.

When we ask the personal question *Why?* about every action we choose, our thinking is awakened to a new level. Remember doing something stupid as a child? Your mom or dad probably asked, "What were you thinking?" The problem was, you were not thinking. The concept of *thinking* first, *choosing* logically, and then *accessing* a new level of energy represents a real application of this old advice.

Thomas Edison once said, "There is no expedient to which a man will not go to avoid the labor of thinking." What he called the labor of thinking, I refer to as an inner conflict. Once you get past the conflict of opposing actions, you attain a harmony through which thinking becomes clearer. Every victory over illogical behavior ignites more energy that transforms thinking patterns and capabilities. The pattern of increased thinking helps identify your personal strengths and purpose or calling in life. This is not a game of denial but of actually unfolding the vast resources of untapped human potential. What could be more exciting?

Free will has always been the key to opening the door to human potential. All the challenges facing the world today need answers from people who are willing to *think* from a new perspective.

We feel compelled to behave illogically. Such behavior is embedded in our nature through our intellectual and emotional makeup. Every time we choose illogical behavior, we deny ourselves the power of freedom. We can choose to remain in a primitive state of existence or to evolve to another reality. This is not religion, morals, or political correctness. My words are a challenge to the planet.

CHAPTER 3

SO WHAT'S LOGICAL?

My experiences with substance use all came to a head late in 1973 when, literally overnight, a lightbulb turned on. I saw my experiment on free choice from a new perspective. I realized that all my choices had been based on feelings. I knew I was human and that emotions were part of the package, but what if emotions were taken out of the equation and free choice was based on logic only? What if I overlooked all my rationalizations for pleasurable behavior?

A NEW APPROACH

This new perception aroused intense emotions within me, and I decided to start a new experiment immediately: I would choose my actions based on logic. Instead of separating emotions from logic, I would find harmony between them. This is where my new life began.

When I realized how illogical it was to ingest alcohol and drugs, something remarkable happened. I stopped the illogical behavior, and my mind started to think! Amazing! It wasn't at all comfortable. During the holiday season, with my abstinence from substances, my mind really got worked up. I looked at my friends, relatives, and acquaintances from a different perspective, and they suddenly viewed me in a different way as well. My usual crowd started alienating themselves from me—a logical response, of course.

I looked at everyone and everything around me, and my perceptions changed. I got that *Star Trek* feeling—as if I were going where no one had gone before! I embraced the changes going on in my mind as an adventure.

As I began to view the world in logical terms, four major changes took place. First, as mentioned above, I stopped ingesting alcohol and other drugs, which opened my mind to a new way of thinking.

Choosing Language

The second change that occurred was a change in my language. With my use of substances, I had developed the habit of using colorful word combinations. Let's just say that the graphic, shocking language of some rappers today is kindergarten talk compared to my language at the time.

While I was using these substances, I felt it was my right or freedom to use any language I wanted. Amazing! But when I engaged my mind in *thinking*, I suddenly realized I had a choice of language. Obscene language, swearing, and the use of profanity or obscene gestures became illogical. Think about it: What is the purpose of language? The answer is communication. What does profane language communicate? The answer is, nothing purposeful, positive, or logical. I chose to remove illogical words and gestures from my efforts to communicate.

Imagine the shock to my system. There I was, stripped of the alcohol and drugs that had been my way of life for five years. There I was, reduced to using only language that is logical and that actually communicates. My brain was really wondering what was going on! I was *thinking*! I felt as if I had rewired my brain, though I didn't understand the sensation at the time.

Every day, I asked myself, *Why am I going through this? I'm losing my friends. This strange, new world is alien to me.* This was just the beginning. My thinking mind was going to unravel me way beyond just weird feelings and a change in perception.

WHAT ABOUT SEX?

The third change was even more shocking. Like most male human beings, I have always been aroused sexually by visual input. Prior to this new awakening from substance use, if I got an erection, masturbation seemed like a normal response. Casual sex with a willing female was acceptable. I indulged in pornography as well. After all, those actions were part of freedom, weren't they? It was my body; I should have been free to pleasure myself, shouldn't I?

When my mind went into thinking mode, I started seeing this activity from a different perspective. It was like studying human anatomy all over again, with new eyes. I became aware that I was choosing to engage in illogical sexual actions. These feelings were difficult and uncomfortable. The metamorphosis triggered by my abstinence from substances was making me see sex differently.

I broke it down to tiny choices that had nothing to do with religion, government, or the morals of society. Questions arose. Why was my penis getting erect, and where did the process start? The process always began in my mind, and it occurred to me that the whole physiology of sex was part of a system of procreation.

So allowing pornography into my mind with the known reaction of sexual arousal was illogical. Therefore, I had to stop feeding my mind with pornography. Stimulating an erection outside of procreation was disrespectful to my very nature.

Is this getting wild or what? In the time of substance use, I viewed all kinds of sexual encounters as my choice and my right. In the sixties, the hippie ideals of free love and the absurdity of marriage imposed no limits on sexual activity. The creation of birth-control pills had taken away the inconvenience of pregnancy.

The choice of heterosexual or homosexual activity was part of the freedom; I could easily have become bisexual or homosexual as part of my pursuit of freedom.

But those choices wouldn't work when I thought about sex in a logical way. The purpose of sex is procreation, not merely self-pleasure. Therefore, logically, sex must be between a male and female who are willing to care for the children they produce.

Strong sexual urges seem to create feelings of love, but the choice to love is far more powerful than the feeling of love. When one chooses to love, harmony in a relationship and sexual intimacy (as an expression of love) are taken to a new level of happiness and satisfaction.

THE POWER OF TRUE FREEDOM

The result of the three changes described above led to the fourth and most important change: I harnessed the power of true freedom. What you cannot see are the changes that were going on in my mind. My perception of the known reality was changing incredibly; my self-esteem and confidence level were increasing dramatically. I was feeling a sense of unbelievable power! I discovered a sense of freedom greater than I could have ever imagined—a freedom with some meat behind it.

I was still aware that I was human and could not avoid all the illogical emotions that are part of being human. I had to find the harmony or peace between the two opposing forces of yin and yang. As time passed by, with quiet thinking and meditation, the pressure and stress calmed down. With my increase of logical thinking, I became more aware of the growing significance of choice.

LOGICAL DECISIONS EQUAL LOGICAL RESULTS

With these four major changes in attitude toward substance use, vulgar language, sex, and the meaning of freedom, I soon noticed two specific results: a thirst for knowledge and a desire to share my new perceptions.

I had finished high school, but my goal had been simply to get out. I disliked reading; it bored me, so I simply managed to get through school without reading anything. What is educational about that? As I changed my choices and my lifestyle, I felt a need to learn. I started to read for fifteen minutes every day—autobiographies or nonfiction titles about science or economics. I still don't like to read, yet I manage to read a book per month because of my craving for knowledge!

Logical choices produce logical results. I wanted knowledge. As I gained knowledge and thought more logically, I felt a powerful surge of confidence. In the past, my emotional choices had produced pleasurable feelings, but they had never produced this kind of growth and confidence.

Saying no to illogical behavior also created in me a compassion for all humans. I wanted to find out why some choices increased my sensation of power and confidence while others, specifically the choices I made during and before substance use, did not. I wanted to share with everyone the power and confidence that I had discovered. This is what compelled me to write about the changes I made.

I believe anybody can achieve the same kind of growth that I have experienced. You can learn to make choices from a state of total freedom, not limited by government, religion, or society. Imagine a world filled with confident, compassionate people who think logically and do not engage in behaviors that might harm others, like war or crime. That's what the power of freedom can produce.

My life is always growing and changing. I have made and continue to make lots of mistakes. I have accepted the reality of being human. Striving for perfection but never being able to achieve it is ultimately the greatest challenge. Can such an endeavor be any different than pursuing happiness without ever quite achieving perfect happiness? Maybe the pursuit, in itself, brings on a feeling of happiness. I sense it has in my own life, for I am very happy and do not fear death.

CHAPTER 4

ILLUSIONS OF THE MIND

All the illusions we have created for ourselves could be the greatest deceptions we face in our time. Making choices based only on feelings, without involving logical thought, may be just as unnatural to our human nature as trying to use only logic. When in history have civilizations advanced by pursuing all the feelings of pleasure without restraint?

AN OBSERVATION

I was visiting a casino in Nevada and noticed some very bizarre behavior. People were playing some kind of a game where they sat in front of a machine and kept putting money into it! What drives them to do that? Is it the chance of winning? Logically the odds are stacked against them, so why continue? Many people engage in this activity, so there must be a reason. Feelings of excitement and energy are created in the game playing.

A related trend in our society is the use of lotteries in different states. The concept of increasing revenues through a game of chance is a way of manipulating and appeasing the public. It is not a matter of figuring the odds of winning. Rather the lottery instills in a society the idea that gaining wealth is a matter of chance or luck. Accepting this philosophy inhibits the powers from within that can realize any dream through freedom. Whether we should participate in the lottery is not a matter of legality but choice. Allowing ourselves to pursue this illusion is illogical.

Gambling is a subtle block to the power of freedom. It blocks the energy required for the tremendous creative potential of the mind to be released. When humans do not realize the undeveloped powers they have inside them, they form a belief in the concept of luck, believing that chance controls and determines destiny. That very illusion can prevent access to the power of freedom. It relieves us of the burden of accountability for our choices. If luck determines the outcome, our behavior makes no difference.

Gambling is fun and pleasurable; otherwise, people wouldn't do it. The problem is that the energy being created doesn't access the power of freedom but in fact prevents it from happening at all. While the gambling behavior continues, the participants have no clue of what is really taking place inside them or of the huge price they are paying for such pleasurable feelings.

Perhaps gambling on our own dormant potential is the greatest thrill of all. Any belief can become a self-created religion, preventing us from seeing reality clearly. It is amazing to observe that an alternate, logical version of all the feel-good activities in our society can be found on the other side of the power of freedom. Our consuming economy would make us believe that all the feel-good experiences are here to be purchased for a price. Ironically, feeling good is as free as the air we breathe. The only price we pay is overcoming our fear of thinking.

Everyone needs to be free to choose his or her actions, and I don't want to sound judgmental. I only offer another perspective on observed behavior. It is only by understanding, and through freedom of choice, that we can get through the initial doorway to the true power of freedom just on the other side. The freedom to choose to gamble cannot be denied. Tremendous energy from within is waiting to be released just behind the self-illusion of gambling.

ENERGY AND CHANGE

Energy is the common denominator—how we create it and what we do with it is specific to individuals and cultures. Many Eastern religions have techniques on how to develop chi, an internal energy that they claim can bring well-being and harmony. I am sure that they have acquired much knowledge of the subject over the centuries. We would be wise to learn from them. But so it is with all the different cultures and societies on the planet. The combined knowledge and wisdom of the world holds many solutions to our planetary challenges. We need to find a common denominator in our communications, free from arrogance.

Our present government has given us the freedom to pursue our dreams, and that simple freedom has created much wealth and satisfaction for many. However, the vast majority of the population doesn't understand or value that simple privilege. As long as the real power of freedom is not understood, the majority of the population will let the current interpretation of freedom fade into history. Our society, now more than ever, needs to form a more perfect union. The goal is to revitalize the meaning of freedom, so all citizens can understand its true value and importance.

This elevated meaning of freedom can spread rather quickly when people see the results in the changed behavior of just a few. Change has to happen. If we miss this opportunity, we may never get another chance. Complacency is not experienced by just the nonthinkers of society, but by those who have benefited from the existing system. Real change will affect everyone. Those who have used the system to their advantage and have found success in their lives will fear change. Organizations that build success through greed and arrogance will have great fear of change. That fear will produce pressure to stop the change in order to eliminate a threat to their financial position.

I heard an interesting statement made by a single woman on welfare: she said money was only paper and had no meaning in her life. Just that kind of statement proves an important principle: that which is not earned is not valued. If we do not teach the true meaning of freedom, and if the masses do not understand it, freedom will lose its value. Until we realize the true power of freedom, freedom in itself will not survive. Freedom cannot stand alone without evolving. Freely pursuing every human pleasure and emotional gratification will never release any power.

Our new interpretations of freedom have created such absurd behavior in our society that it enrages the fundamentalist Islamic groups. These groups have no concept of the power of freedom, perhaps partly because our society is presently not portraying it very well. We have today two opposing forces that engage in illogical behavior. On September 11, 2001, a terrorist named Osama Bin Laden attacked the United States; a few months later, we attacked Saddam Hussein in Iraq! In religious fervor, terrorists commit suicide and take innocent lives with them in the name of Allah. Does this behavior sound logical on either side? Both sides rationalize their behavior in support of their actions.

My perspective on current events demands so much daily patience, because I realize that during my five-year experiment in substance use, I could have rationalized so many absurd behaviors in my own actions—all in the name of freedom. I was there in the sixties and got caught up in all the revelry and rebellion for change in the name of freedom. Someone has to shed light on a specific time in history when a single generation started misinterpreting the meaning of freedom. It was a time when change was needed and many questions were raised. *Why?* was the biggest question.

Trying to find solutions while consuming a new lineup of substances only created a whole new altered array of problems. It is not the existence of substances that is at issue here, but how they are integrated into our pursuit of happiness in the name of freedom. The more our society believes its people have the right to feel good regardless of the means, the more the path to the doorway to the power of freedom is hidden in absurdity.

Our forefathers have paid a tremendous price for this experiment in freedom called the United States of America. When our constitution was being created, an assembly of courageous people risked death as revolutionaries, yet they engaged in the best thinking at the time. They analyzed known governments from Europe and attempted to remove as many flaws from their systems as possible to create a more perfect union.

"We the People" still have the power to re-create our system today to a more perfect union. This is not a pie-in-the-sky dream or a metaphysical, surrealistic fantasy; it is a down-to-earth, reawakening approach to freedom that any citizen can practice.

In the last thirty years, I have come across many space-shot ideas on how we can all arrive at nirvana and heavenly bliss. I have to wonder what kind of acid such theorists consumed in their lifetime. They all had their feet planted in some distant universe with no earthly relevance. If you are wondering whether a doorway to the power of freedom exists and if is it possible to live on that path, well, I exist in that freedom, and it is possible.

EMBRACING THE UNCOMFORTABLE

One of the challenges any new idea encounters is the odd feeling of being different. There is a strong tendency among humans in social groups to keep everyone on the same page of thinking. This intellectual accord is like a security blanket people create to feel comfortable and accepted. Stepping out will be uncomfortable, but so what? What is so comfortable about the state of our society today? Have our relationships gotten any better? Are our children smarter or better educated or more secure? Is our economic system functioning more equitably? What comfort can we find in pursuing the same old-same old?

If you have read this far, you have the power to change to become more. Failure to act with sufficient evidence is illogical. When you strip away the facade of what we are really capable of, there are no excuses. Everyone, whether from Appalachia or Harvard, can begin the journey to significance.

All people will have a price to pay, but so what? We are all paying a price for insignificance! Taking thinking to a new level will expose the absurdity of our society's behavior. When our eyesight is bad, we have no problem going to the optometrist. Why would you not want to see better? Facing reality is not easy; it is scary. But what is the alternative? We must be vigilant about how we spend the dash between the dates on our tombstones. How can we live an entire lifetime and never clearly see reality for what it is? Do we want to ignore our potential and live only at a survival level?

Where in a free society do we find the standard for discipline? This is where the concept of free choice based on logic becomes relevant. Logic challenges our intellect and emotions, simultaneously producing energy. That energy transforms and evolves our thinking to a new level, making a new perspective apparent. Try it—and tell me that you do not sense the energy!

The greatest form of slavery that exists in our society today is slavery to illogical behavior. I could list many examples: people disrespecting one another in marriages, the use of vulgar language, substance use, and gambling, to name a few. We make all kinds of rationalized excuses, and still the slavery continues! Are we in the land of the free or what? All this slavery blocks access to the real power of freedom. We have such a primitive concept of freedom that the real power stays hidden from our reality.

The tension that you feel when you make a choice based on logic is normal. The energy that choice creates must be allowed to do its magic in your mind. The rewiring of thinking patterns will feel weird, but it's okay! The evolution of mankind is only going to take place within humans who become aware and choose to make the change. This evolution will not ever take place simply because centuries have gone by. We, as a species, may be standing more erect than our ancestors, but time alone will not release the powers that already exist in the mind.

Our technology is no comparison to the marvels yet to be realized in the human mind. Our technology has nothing to do with the evolution from within that needs to take place. Our petty interpretations of freedom and legal rationalizations are not leading our species to any higher level of thought. Our current civilization shows no improvement in the quality of life as a whole. Educational systems are failing, general health is poorer, and relationships are less stable. Show me the improvement in our society since the sixties! As I mentioned in the beginning, the only way to effectively change an idea is to replace it with a better idea.

This book is a challenge to humankind that real life-altering change from within is possible at the deepest level. We all possess incredible gifts that need to be awakened. For some of us, the existing systems have made it possible to explore and expand some of our gifts, but with the awakening of more people, we can improve current governmental, educational, and social systems to new and higher standards. Our basic understanding of freedom serves only as a catalyst for releasing the power of freedom.

When in Doubt, Choose the Difficult

Sometimes we have a problem with defining what is logical. Some may say, "What's illogical to you seems logical to me." While there may be situations that would fit that statement, it sounds like rationalization to me. Generally, I find that the logical choice of action is almost always the most difficult one. This observation cannot be ascertained as an absolute, but if logic is in question, making the more difficult choice of action should be correct. These energy-producing ideas create change from within and will accelerate humankind's evolution to greatness.

Maybe our physical changes in the course of our evolution happened because of environmental changes or out of need for basic survival, and time was all that was required. The marvels of the human intellect will not be released by accident; time will not simply erode away our foolishness. We must become aware of the doorway that we must pass through to reach another realm. This realm is what I call "The New Age of Enlightenment." Noticing bizarre behavior is easy when you are sensitive to it. Just picture a college professor or a doctor smoking a cigarette. That behavior would be defined as illogical and yet even with the knowledge of the dangers involved, the behavior continues. Education in itself does not release the power of freedom. Education can exercise some of the brain's functions, but it does not release the power of freedom. The rewiring of thinking patterns eliminates old paradigms, so educational systems can be taken to new highs. Brilliance is taking known information and applying it to new spheres of thinking. There are many dormant brilliant minds out there that may never enter the classical educational system. Yet they may be holding the answers to the challenges humankind is facing today!

All the challenges we are facing today have a lot to do with illogical choices that we as a society have made through the years. Think of how much conflict just the slavery issue has caused. When our country was being formed on principles of freedom and equality, there existed the practice of slavery. Our constitution eventually exposed the flaws in a system that accepted slavery. Stating that humans are created equal with inalienable rights created a dilemma. We are still struggling with this one idea. Our laws and their applications are still not perfect. Our pursuit of a more perfect union continues!

Abolishing slavery was a very difficult and costly change that took place at the time of the Civil War. Change is possible! Logic will eventually win out. The vastness of the human mind and potential cannot be eternally denied! Slavery to our old thinking patterns will eventually be exposed for what it is. Our survival as a species on this planet depends on it. Yet some will continue to claim that expanding the interpretation of freedom to promote illogical behavior is going to advance civilization. I say, "Show me the energy that is released by indulging in illogical behavior. Where is thinking ignited to new dimensions?"

The effect of not doing an activity has to be of greater real value than the effect of doing an activity. People need tangible results to sink their teeth into. Pleasure is a strong motivator, but so is the release and sensation of energy. If freedom is used as license only for immediate gratification or pleasure, the power of freedom is never realized. Our drive for pleasure is a barrier that needs to be crossed.

Through the development of our medical technology in the field of sex and reproduction, we have been able to separate sexual pleasure from any connection to procreation. The subsequent rationalization of its singular use as the pleasurable right of the individual is altering our social structure at its core. This change in our society is responsible for a whole array of illogical behavior, including same-sex marriage and pornography, as discussed earlier. Here is where we get some colorful rationalizations regarding alternate lifestyles and love. When logical choices are made, a sense of tension usually occurs. The same tension occurs at first with illogical choices, but it disappears with rationalization. The human conscience has magnetism toward logical behavior, but our present concept of freedom, our medical professionals, and our legal systems are working together to create an illusion of guilt-free, illogical behavior.

The same applies to all illogical behavior. At first, a sense of guilt appears, and we cannot continue the activity without getting rid of the guilt. Maybe that original guilt has a higher purpose than just to annoy us. When the slave business got started, did slave traders see the African natives as human? What kind of rationalization did they use to get rid of any guilt that came up in their pursuit of profit? What a price human history has paid and continues to pay for just that one rationalization of illogical behavior.

Could it be that we humans today condone illogical activity if it is profitable? Do we label as logical anything that brings us profit? Do we believe that profit justifies itself? That opens up a whole new bag of tricks! Can you see where we, as a society, need to change our thinking patterns in order to begin addressing the issues of today?

Radical Muslims say the solution is to kill everybody who doesn't join their belief system. Killing is illogical! Making sense out of nonsense has always been a great human flaw. Finding harmony between the emotions and the intellect has never been easy for us. That is why we need to take baby steps in unraveling the confusion. The journey has to start with eliminating substance use or any illogical behavior. Then we can change our thinking patterns and release the power of freedom.

THE ILLUSION OF ARROGANCE

We in America have a head start with our understanding of freedom, but other governments around the world also have good concepts in their understanding of human nature. We could learn from these governments as we form a more perfect union. Unfortunately, we Americans often think we are better, stronger, and smarter than the rest of the world. This attitude is arrogance at its worst. We need to discard arrogant, prideful attitudes and other illusions that prevent us from thinking logically and cooperating with diverse cultures.

When I started using logic as the basis of choice, my perception changed. I saw people as no different than myself, except for the choices they made. Arrogance is an illusion that separates people into supposedly superior or inferior groups. It would be comical if it weren't so tragic. When we view other people as our inferiors, we waste their potential and our own.

Arrogance never was an effective means of influencing other nations. On the contrary, it is probably the single most antagonizing attitude in human relations. With our current fiscal and social challenges, we cannot afford to be arrogant.

In addition, our flaws are sometimes better seen from outside our country. If we can set aside our pride long enough to see ourselves from outside our borders, the process has a chance to begin. Our constitution was written for the people, and "We the

People" have to prove that we can take our freedom to the next level of evolution.

Arrogance is not only a political issue but also a personal issue. The emotion of pride blurs the individual's vision of reality. Pride can mask illogical behavior just as effectively as any other misguided emotion. Here are some real examples of pride at work on a personal level.

- A husband's pride in being a good provider for his family may lead him to rationalize extramarital affairs or substance consumption.
- A worker's pride in being effective and reliable may cause him to rationalize substance use—but only on weekends.
- Our own illusion of status, however it is created, can cause rationalization of an amazing array of illogical behavior—from the supposedly proper use of substance use to the out-of-focus perception of other people.

Arrogance comes from the self-created illusion of grandeur. So just as arrogance can prevent countries from finding solutions to their differences, arrogance in a society can prevent people from uniting together for a common cause. When a free people take that freedom to a new level, arrogance disappears. Then arrogance is perceived as the illusion that it really is.

ILLUSIONS VERSUS REALITY

While emotions are an essential part of being human, making choices based solely on emotions creates illusions that cripple our ability to solve problems. I see many cultural changes taking place, all because feelings are given priority over logical analysis. Thinking is being replaced by emotions even in our legal systems. We try to legislate things like self-esteem or sexual preference. By prioritizing feelings, we accept bizarre behavior as normal, and we condemn normal behavior as prejudice!

Under the illusion of freedom and compassion, our American culture is gradually accepting absurd choices. We describe freedom as the omnipotent virtue and claim unrestrained pleasure as our birthright. We exhibit a false compassion for people who make illogical choices in their illogical pursuit of happiness. Legal professionals are invoking the concept that denying self-pleasure is unhealthy and detrimental! Loopholes are being found to substantiate these claims, so laws will not interfere with desires. When these absurd loopholes are challenged, our Supreme Court upholds them, rationalizing everything in the name of individual freedom. Unbelievable!

Let me give another example. When the great American Civil War took place, much blood was shed to keep the union united under one flag. There existed at the time two separate cultures with undeniable differences. A little over a hundred years later, we find another threat to a unified, multicultural nation. For reasons unknown, the Spanish language has been given preferential status over all the other languages of American citizens. Why do all immigrants have to learn English to obtain citizenship except one group? Why? Is it because we consider this culture incapable of learning?

Through a misunderstanding of the Constitution and the implementation of bizarre exceptions, "We the People" are creating a dual society. What happened to one nation? Was the Civil War fought and reconciled so that the nation could be split again 150 years later? My French-speaking parents had to learn English to obtain their drivers' licenses. All documentation was in English. Why wasn't it offered in French?

Does it take a genius to see that with the Spanish birth rate far exceeding all other nationalities, our system of government could vote to choose Spanish as the common language and require everyone to learn it? How about "Press two for English," for starters? Why are these exceptions continuing, and for what purpose? Officially establishing English as the national common language would only be acknowledging what the general population already knows.

The unleashing of the power of freedom will slowly clear the fog of illusions; then everyone can perceive a new vision. As the old saying goes, "You can't hit a target if you cannot see it!" Unfortunately, removing the fog is just what our society fears. We are comfortable in our self-created boxes of complacency. We need the courage to change. There is actually nothing to fear, because fear is also an illusion. Action makes the fear disappear!

We must remove the veil of illusions now, at this crucial time in history. Without a new vision, we will not be able to solve the massive challenges facing the planet.

During my experimentation with substance use, I found myself immersed in many illusions I created for myself. I was almost overtaken by these illusions.

My experience is no different from other people coming of age and trying to discover who they are. The difference is that people who discover themselves through a similar path have accepted an illusion of who they are! Somewhere in the metamorphosis, they forfeited their incredible capacity to think and became incapable of thinking outside the box of their own illusions. This is why change from within is so difficult. Our illusions of who we are control us, stripping us of the real power of freedom.

My story proves change is possible, and there is nothing to fear. Even a false belief can make an illusion seem real. Freedom gives us choice; so much power is hidden just beyond the illusion!

CHOOSING REALITY

When as I began choosing a different way of life, it became more noticeable to me that people all around me were embracing the illusions they created through the use of various substances. From my perspective, people who choose what feels good without conscious thought are creating a society indulging in bizarre behavior.

Why do so many people repeat behavior that they know produces undesirable results? Why do they accept results they don't want? They don't *think*. Shortly after I made the changes in my behavior, and even today, my family and friends wondered why I changed. My answer, which always confuses them, is that I *chose* to change.

Given my French-Quebec background, alcohol use is as natural as the air we breathe. The choices I made conflicted with my cultural past. Some say a person can't change because of genetic traits or chemistry. This is a false argument. It is easier to say "I can't stop drinking" than to *choose* to stop. The majority of people who use substances to feel good are not mentally ill. They like to feel good, and they don't want to change. So they make excuses and blame some other factor: genetics, family habits, the devil—whatever illusion they can blame for their illogical behavior.

To say that our race is doomed to stupid, repetitive behavior for whatever reason is illogical. "We the People" must stop blaming illusions and take responsibility for our actions. We must find the courage to exercise the mental muscle to try again after a failure. People confuse the pursuit of excellence with being perfect; humans cannot become perfect. Some people rationalize that because perfection cannot be achieved, the pursuit of excellence is futile. This is another illusion that keeps us from going through the first doorway of freedom to the power of freedom, which transforms us to something greater.

Choosing to access the power of freedom gives true equality to all mankind. There are no man-made limitations, no diplomas, no authorities that can deny you. This equality is truly your birthright. Every human who *chooses* to do so can move to a higher level of consciousness and intelligence.

When you begin to think in a new way, you cannot imagine how building from one logical decision to another can change your whole perception of reality. As your perception of the world around you changes, the absurdity of human behavior will become more obvious.

The mother of famous neurosurgeon Dr. Ben Carson used to tell him to see beyond what he already saw in his mind. His insight into the human brain's potential is amazing. Dr. Carson was fortunate enough to become aware of his personal gifts through his awakening thirst for knowledge. Like Dr. Carson, all people have unique gifts, and each has a particular journey to travel. This uniqueness makes all of us important and valuable to the survival and evolution of mankind.

If we continue to hide behind the illusions we've created, horrendous consequences will occur. Unless we conquer our fears, they will defeat us. Most people are afraid of dying; they also fear living a life without enjoying its pleasures. But perhaps the fear of change is the greatest fear of all, even if we believe that the change will bring us to something greater than our illusions.

I watched a documentary on the people of the Appalachian Mountains. These people are no different from you or me, except for choices they have made. Tremendous poverty exists among the people in Appalachia; the area is filled with trash and run-down houses. When asked why they don't move to a better place, the typical interviewee answered, "This is home." This is a vivid example of a minisociety living on emotion, rather than thinking through the problems. Even there in the mountains, the power of freedom would change their lives, but their fear of the unknown is too great to allow them to break the complacency.

That may be an extreme example, but most of us have a comfort zone that supports our lifestyle. We don't realize that unless we face the challenges and solve the problems, our lifestyle will be affected even more dramatically—and sometimes negatively. Imagine vast numbers of vacated, bankrupt business properties with trash everywhere because towns cannot pay for rubbish removal. Imagine the threat to public safety if we can't pay for an adequate police force. The collapse of our economic systems will change the American landscape and lifestyle.

THE ENEMY WITHIN

The attack on Pearl Harbor shows what can happen when a great power is caught sleeping. We are under attack by an enemy from within today. Are we going to be caught sleeping in our complacency?

Make no mistake about it: the enemy is within. Banks, financial institutions, and corporations are made up of a lot of individuals who are arrogantly complacent, accepting the primitive illusions they have created. Arrogance doesn't release the power of freedom. Credibility through academic credentials alone doesn't validate superior intelligence; any amount of knowledge, no matter how vast, can be limited by small thinking. Snobbery or arrogance are feelings of superiority that can be developed in many ways. It seems to appear mostly when a people sense they have arrived at some point of significance in their lives. Real thinking ceases, and personal growth stops. It could be an academic degree or an occupational level. Somewhere in their personal choices of behavior, most people are blocking access to their true potential. Degrees and job positions do not go deep enough to address one's personal choices to engage in illogical behavior. There are some brilliant thinkers out there, but they may not be in the government or corporate boardrooms.

The enemy we are facing, unfortunately, cannot be faced on the battlefield. The enemy we face is staring at us in the mirror, hiding behind the complacent fog that we have created for ourselves. A battle must be waged if we are to succeed, but it must come from within each individual.

A harmony exists between the two opposing forces when we break free to the power of freedom. We must fight for that harmonious line of peace between the yin and yang. The battle will not be an illusion. Real pain and fear must be overcome, just as in a physical battlefield.

Do we Americans have the courage and determination to stand up to this challenge? The fear of the consequences of defeat should be enough to inspire us. Think of the future our children's children will have unless we act. I am reaching out in these words to people who are ready to start real change from within by releasing the true power of freedom.

My sense of urgency has awakened in the last five years. The time for action is upon us now. Mankind has reached an apex that demands massive change on a planetary level. The free world, led by the United States, needs to start these internal changes. Will history witness fear and complacency eluding the change from within, eventually leading to our own destruction? Our nation's credibility to the rest of the world will greatly improve when the true energy of the power of freedom is released. Our wealth is far beyond just our natural resources and capital. Our greatest asset is the diversity of our people and cultures and the tremendous power within every citizen.

Until mankind unleashes the true power of freedom, we will always fall short of our potential.

Each of us has the key to change the future, one personal choice at a time. No one gets lost in insignificance. No one is less important than another human being, so no one can hide under the illusion that participation in the evolution is not important. We can no longer hide behind all the illusions that we have created for ourselves over the centuries.

CHAPTER 5

CHANGE FROM WITHIN

The old Chinese philosophy of the yin and yang shows that a harmony can exist between two opposing forces. Somehow our modern societies seem to say that the freedom to pursue happiness warrants any choice that makes you feel good. It is like accepting only the yin in the equation to avoid the tension that naturally exists between opposites.

We cannot deny emotions from human nature any more than we can deny the existence of the intellect or mind. We can't expect to release the true potential of every human being without first accepting the fact of the existence of both emotion and intellect. Humans are complex; we are influenced by outside forces, and we often become enslaved to them, but we don't have to remain in slavery. Any change that we desire has to come from our freedom of choice, and that is *not* an outside force. To access the power of freedom, we must change from within.

Perhaps you are thinking, *I don't use alcohol or drugs, and I never have. I already practice married sex only, and I work hard to control my language. What else do I need to do?*

While substance use, casual sex, and bad language are among the most obvious illogical behaviors, there are many more to consider. Some require deeper thought and more complicated changes than others. Think of all the choices we have the liberty of making every day that can be just as controversial and difficult as those listed earlier.

How about the ever-popular choice of abortion? That one issue causes so many emotions in our society to flare up. Can you feel the emotions of a pregnant female who doesn't want to be pregnant? Very powerful feelings! Difficult decisions! If you remove the feelings from the equation, is it logical to terminate a life because it will make you feel better? Other solutions could be found with thought and feeling. It is amazing that in our freedom to pursue happiness, many humans choose the yin and avoid acceptance of the yang.

Albert Einstein's definition of insanity, which is "doing the same thing over and over again and expecting different results," seems appropriate here. It is almost as if humanity has been held back from development to a higher state of existence by the force of fear. Mix in a good dose of social or religious false ideas, and bingo, you have a history of mankind repeating the same mistakes and essentially staying the same as a species. Now that's crazy!

Remember that during my in-depth, five-year experiment with the use of various substances, my very perception of society and reality was altered considerably. Again, the results of this study are not to be confused with an argument about what is moral behavior or what constitutes right and wrong. Maybe the human ego or vanity develops simultaneously as a society matures, creating a box where the masses of people feel safe and no longer feel the need to think. The individuals who do engage in thinking today are probably just as amazed as I am at the historic illogical behavior of mankind as a whole.

My attitude and behavior at the time of the experiment was entirely different from what it is today. The difference now is that I understand why such behavior exists. In the final phase of the five-year experiment, I became aware of all the different people I could have become. The effects of different substances showed me many illusions of my ego.

THE SPIRITUAL

So far, I have acknowledged the obvious existence of man's physical body and intellect. I cannot continue without discussing the very real existence of the spiritual part of the human condition. I could have avoided this topic except for the fact that living in harmony with two opposing forces constantly requires tapping into the power of another force, called the spiritual force or higher power.

This is a difficult subject, because freedom requires that belief in the spiritual be a choice of free will. All humans must be free to believe or not in a higher power. This brings a whole new topic of discussion to the forefront. The history of humankind is interlaced with religion and cultural beliefs. Opening the door through freedom to the sleeping greatness in every person requires some kind of support system from a higher power. Forces do exist, whether spiritual or man-made, that do not want "We the People" to become aware of our inert potential. Those forces need to be kept at bay by accessing a greater power.

I am not going to discuss my personal beliefs or tell you what you should or shouldn't believe. I will try to explain what the parameters of any belief system should be. That belief system could be personal or part of some organized religion or congregation. It must not deny free will of choice. Remember, whenever free will is not present in our choices, the potential for power or energy being derived is eliminated. Any personal belief or religion that through brainwashing deadens or eliminates that awareness of free choice should be avoided.

A belief system must recognize the greatness and importance of every human being. The Constitution of the United States recognizes the equality of all people. Each person has a unique purpose in which exists the happiness and fulfillment of life. The

Constitution acknowledges this fundamental right to the pursuit of happiness.

The purpose for mentioning this topic is not to claim that I am an expert, but it would be a disservice not to discuss it, because it is part of the whole story. I do not know if it is possible to pursue a life in the manner I have been describing without the spiritual aspect.

This spiritual awareness is not unique to me. In our society, all kinds of old and new beliefs, religions, and philosophies exist. Many people claim to have a stairway to heaven. I am not qualified to render any judgment here. It seems that when a society loses its vision for a brighter future, more people appear to offer a drug or a belief that will make everything better. Some claim that following a certain diet or abstaining from certain foods will lead to a long, healthy life. Some people become very concerned about certain animals becoming extinct or being abused. It is not that these ideas or concerns are unimportant, but these activities seem to be a reaction to other realities in their life that don't make sense.

Placing a strong focus on these singular ideas or problems eases the tension of living in an illogical world. To me, it shows the tremendous energies being held at bay by so many people simply because they greatly fear the realities of the total picture. I have met many people who focus so much on one singular idea or belief that their feet seem to leave the ground. When they put their efforts toward finding a feel-good existence, their genius does not contribute to the improvement of mankind, and that seems like an unfortunate waste. All this behavior that is exhibited all over the world plainly shows that mankind is thirsting and yearning to grow and develop to a higher state of being.

Are we, as a society, going to let destruction blindside us? I couldn't help but watch a TV documentary on cosmetic surgery. The number of people who have cosmetic surgery may be only a minute segment of our society, but the fact that we participate in this madness at all is an example of just how far our illusions of reality have taken us. Our inherent worth is light-years beyond our physical appearance. During my five-year experiment, I remember well trying to find the right combinations of drugs to create the self-image that would give me confidence, but that was an illusion.

Using surgery or any other means to alter one's self-image is another by-product of nonthinking. Thinking would require a human to question the reason for the dissatisfaction with personal appearance. A spiritual element may also help in this area, as a more spiritually fulfilled person is less likely to become so focused on physical attributes.

Our creative ability to avoid thinking and live in an illusionary world is really incredible. From my perspective, it seems completely foolish for any person not to cross the self-imposed barriers and ignite his or her power of freedom. An enormous amount of energy is available to help one lose weight or learn to accept one's appearance or make any other needed change.

That energy may feel different or uncomfortable at first, but the effects begin immediately. When the initial decision to change a behavior occurs, all the focus is on the feelings the new choice produces. That's the period of time when the brain is being rewired. It is probably best not to make any more behavioral changes until you have adapted this new choice into your life.

We all engage in some activity that blocks out thinking. I would recommend starting with the more blatant activity and then working on the smaller issues. This process is a lifelong journey to perfection that is never fully attained but always pursued. This pursuit can make life an adventure, which eliminates the possibility of boredom.

The whole process has another by-product, and that is an increase of personal strength of character. The best way I can describe it is the "Rocky effect," or a person's ability to get up after being knocked down! That resilience is the stuff this country was built on. The more of it we have as a nation, the more grit we have to overcome challenges facing us. This "Rocky effect" is the essence of what makes a country strong. It is a source of courage to undertake the seemingly impossible tasks. Doesn't it sound like something we need today?

The genius of humanity exists not only in a few rare individuals; it resides in every person on the planet. We may have significant differences, but we are all important. If a society elevates its vision of the future, hope is awakened, and hope ignites belief, which produces action. That immediate action has never been more needed than it is today. In true freedom, everyone can find his or her purpose for existence.

It is only in a free society that one can find that purpose, but it still remains an inside job. You have to discover that purpose for yourself! It is there, plain as can be, just beyond the illusions. Even after more than thirty-five years of living in this freedom, I still make mistakes. The heightened activity of my mind caused by increased energy doesn't eliminate error. But I also recognize the error much sooner, accept its occurrence, and learn from it.

LIKE-MINDED GROUPS

The tempering of human emotions is another by-product of pursuing the power of freedom. It is not and cannot be an elimination of emotions but rather an elevation of compassion. It is natural for humans to unite in groups around shared ideas or beliefs. However, many like-minded groups of people base their primitive thinking on a foundation of flighty and unstable emotions; in turn, they produce foolish behavior. It is like watching a circus in which only clowns get into the act. They generate a lot of activity, but what's the point?

These like-minded groups could be gangs, social clubs, or self-created religious organizations. Perhaps like-minded people can validate certain behavior with a vote of confidence from their peers. This very behavior is evidence that humans feel a need to justify illogical behavior but are also fearful of dealing with issues in the light of real freedom.

Our free society allows us to choose our actions and our substances. Without that freedom of choice, legal or otherwise, the power or energy that can be found through logical behavior would not exist. I have an enormous amount of feeling and compassion, but I do not have the right to judge or dictate the behavior of another person. Patience is the only solution to enduring so much irrational behavior.

Remember that boredom is one of the causes of complacency, and complacency is an attitude that destroys from within. Within is exactly where the changes have to occur. If "We the People" do not act on our own behalf, the few of power and greed will gladly take control of our lives. This will occur with our own consent in exchange for a sense of security. The illusions of our own thinking will allow this to happen without a fight. The grand experiment in civilization called the United States of America will cease to exist with barely a whimper. We can't let this happen on our watch.

A PROBLEM TO PONDER

Our society's fear of overpopulating the earth with humans has rationalized our reduction of the size of our families. We might think that having fewer people is a good idea, but when all the baby boomers retire, we will have a much smaller workforce to support the financial system. We have created a huge challenge for ourselves that must be met in the next few years. Many of these fiscal problems can no longer be rolled forward to future generations.

The economy of the future will have to find a solution that distributes wealth equitably across the whole human race. Communism has already failed because a few people at the top controlled all facets of work and productivity. To discard the positive effects of free enterprise would be as naive as believing we could give every person an equal share of the wealth. The answer is simple: for wealth to flow to everyone, everyone must participate in its creation.

Upholding this principle involves more than being sure that everyone has a job. Simply having a job that requires little more than showing up and putting in time can hardly be called participating in the creation of wealth. Releasing the power of freedom can also enhance human ability for creating new wealth and creating a better system for sharing the wealth. When masses of people start engaging their minds at a higher level of thinking, abandoning their previous dormant complacency, they will form relationships and cooperate for mutual benefit in the creation of new enterprises. The divisions between businesses and labor factions would dissolve and become irrelevant.

Thinking humans working together for mutual benefit will be crucial to the success of any future economic systems. The use of people for profit has always been a weakness of capitalism. Expecting our current form of primitive capitalism or our government to take care of people who can't or won't work is incredibly naive and ignorant at the very least. Expecting compensation without some form of performance amounts to communism in a fairy-tale world.

The general population has to begin the process by elevating its thinking to a new and unexplored level. That process, along with education about financial intelligence, will have to work simultaneously for the economic system of the future to develop. There is and never was such a thing as a free lunch. This doesn't mean that all human beings on the planet cannot maintain an adequate quality of life. Why is it that the have-nots often seem willing to do more to achieve success than the haves, who always want more but are not willing to *do* more?

Our global economy is sounding a strong wake-up call to any society who has lost its hunger to perform and compete. Anyone who understands the rules of the game can create wealth. Capitalism as we know it today will change as the thinking of the population changes. Capitalism functions far more equitably when all people are treated equally, with dignity and respect.

Mix fiscal problems with drugs and the sexual confusion, and you can see why our society is in danger of failing. Yet society continues to pressure people to remain on the same senseless path: the pursuit of pleasure.

Recently, I heard an interview with a porn star on television. She was young, famous, and open about her sexuality. She freely accepted the pleasures of sex as her right and the pursuit of that pleasure as natural. She and many others like her, male and female, will always be stuck in the illogical and destructive pursuit of pleasure. Our media today eagerly communicates the porn star's message across a wide population. She is spreading an idea or concept that completely blocks access to the true power of freedom.

Sexual misinterpretation has one of the most adverse effects on our society. It breaks down the functioning family unit. Abuse in marriage is common because of the terrific pressures and unrealistic expectations in the average marital relationship. Yet I have found sexual activity within the intimacy of marriage to be far more satisfying than any experiences I encountered during the five-year experiment. I was surprised by this discovery, but I shouldn't have been; sexual and emotional satisfaction within marriage is the logical result when choices are made from true freedom.

Thirty-five years after the sexual revolution of the sixties, can we say that sexual intimacy has improved? Those who pursue happiness by seeking sexual nirvana have created an incredible illusion about the freedom of sexual activity. Actually, thirty-five years of so-called sexual enlightenment have not produced more happiness or satisfaction. Mick Jagger of the Rolling Stones complained in song, "I can't get no satisfaction," and that is still a frustrating dilemma!

Sexual drive is naturally strong, and its purpose is to produce offspring. Its intimacy can be elevated to a higher plane when we begin to realize more and more the true potential of humankind and break through to the power of freedom. Satisfaction comes from the mind, and when thinking begins and increases, that thinking will find gratification.

IMAGINE ...

I have outlined the major problems we face today. Now I challenge you to consider the pathway to solving these problems. Imagine a world in which most people decided to follow the path to true freedom based on making logical, rather than emotional, choices.

- Imagine these people *thinking* clearly and creatively because their minds are not clouded with the destructive effects of alcohol and other drugs.
- Imagine strong, healthy families resulting from the replacement of "free sex" with the satisfying intimacy and procreation found in marriage.
- Imagine cooperation among various races, cultures, and age groups strengthening because each person seeks what is best for all people instead of trying to satisfy selfish desires.
- Imagine a higher standard of living for all people evolving once all people participate in the creation and distribution of wealth.

In such a world, the porn star, the drunk, or the drug addict would be perceived as the oddball—the one who is enslaved to the false freedom of destructive substances and illogical behaviors. Prosperity, not poverty, would be the normal way of life. Then we would truly have a New Age of Enlightenment, because we would use our collective energy and creativity to solve our problems.

I believe I have an obligation to society to write these words, no matter what the outcome. I know my life has had a positive effect on some people, and what more could I ask? I believe that a lot of people are asking the same question I asked: *Why?* I have been asking why all my life, looking for answers that simply make sense among all the nonsense. I cannot stand idly by and do nothing. That would be simply wrong!

Some people don't feel a need to fix society around them as long as everything is okay in their lives. Yet society desperately needs to be fixed. So now is my time to speak up and encourage everyone to seek true freedom, even though that means making difficult choices.

I am sure that these ideas are not what many want to hear. It's like someone coming in and breaking up the party and telling everyone it's time to go home. That's not much fun at first thought.

The excitement begins once initial changes become more comfortable. Our minds are designed to think in a certain way that you will discover when you access the power of freedom. Trust me, you'll be thinking in ways you can't even imagine now, because you will be free from rationalization, guilt, boredom, and complacency.

If we value our freedom, changing our behavior from within will release a tremendous energy that will resound around the world. Our country's greatest curse can be turned into its greatest source of power and serve as a pivotal point of change in our society.

Can we afford to bask in this illusion we have created for ourselves while watching the greatest experiment in self-government fail right before our eyes? Are we so complacent that we are going to let this all go down without even a fight? I cannot believe this!

Our country has faced many challenges, including civil war, and we have survived and prospered. This time, however, the battle needs to be fought from within, and no one will be spared the burden of effort or the reward of success. What makes the United States a great proving ground for the rest of the world is that our society is a superblend of many cultures under one government. If we can show the world that a self-governing, multicultural people can find solutions to their problems, the rest of the world has a chance to get over its petty differences.

It is my compulsion at this time in my life to do whatever it takes to get the message out. We have been on the brink of disaster before in our history. The Cuban missile crisis was a close call, but that event did not require the people of the country to come together to resolve the problem, as with our current issues. Today, some people who see the storm coming are preparing for the worst by arming themselves for protection from anarchy and chaos. These people think small; they lack vision.

Others are embezzling from companies and the government as a means of financial protection from the collapse of our society. These individuals are also prisoners of their small thinking, for they do not see or believe that a solution exists.

Vision for a nation is critically important for sustained development. That vision needs to be nourished with an influx of new ideas from outside of the paradigm of thinking that has brought us to this time in history. Restricting thinking to ancient concepts is not going to make our move into the future happen more quickly.

The mere discovery of new substances that alter our mood or make us feel good is not an advancement of our civilization. Rationalizing new and natural substances that produce the feel-good effect is ludicrous at best. The power of freedom is not going to be released with a new pill or substance; we have plenty of those available right now!

We must redefine freedom, as I stated in the beginning. For me, as for so many others, freedom once meant doing whatever I felt like doing. Only at the end of my five-year experiment did I realize the greater meaning, the greater power available just beyond the obvious. Far beyond the dream of financial or personal success, the gateway to a new world, a New Age of Enlightenment filled with heroes, awaits us.

Adults must begin to make the change from within, demonstrating the power of freedom. Young people who need something to believe in must look to adults as the examples to follow in finding and using the power of true freedom. Then the birth of vision can take place.

Current challenges have us so focused on problems facing our society that our vision is blurred. The stage is set for dramatic change to take place in our society today. Is it so hard to imagine a world where people freely choose not to use substances and release the power of freedom? What kind of world are we creating for the future in these United States of America? If change from within does not occur, aren't the statistics self-evident? The flaws of the system are being exposed. Real freedom changes our perception of reality and engages our thinking to unrealized heights.

CHAPTER 6

The Meaning of Freedom

What does freedom mean? What does freedom have to do with you and me? When I was young, freedom meant doing whatever I felt like doing. In the sixties, we used the phase "doing my thing."

I feel compelled to write this book, because I discovered a hidden power in freedom and how it manifests tremendous energy. This untapped energy can transform the human mind and body.

Our planet is facing many challenges never before seen in history. The solutions to the challenges facing mankind already exist in the most powerful resource on the planet: human beings! The problem is that the vast majority of humans do not realize the powers within.

The power of freedom lies dormant, hidden in our unique ability to choose. A few so-called gifted individuals cannot solve all our planet's problems. Gang members, the homeless, minorities and majorities, the rich and the poor—all are needed, and all are important.

Einstein, Edison, and many great thinkers of the past and present have said that we humans use only a fraction of our brains and potential. So how do we open this door to the human potential? Throughout history, we have tried many methods, including different kinds of government, religion, and education, yet the problems persist and grow.

Those in the powerful and wealthy class encourage people to try the same old solutions, because they want to maintain their power. They would prefer that a large majority of the population stay uninformed and medicated in one way or another so that they can be easily manipulated. Unfortunately, no one wants to admit that the solutions to the problems on our planet rest in the untapped minds and hearts of this vast majority.

The United States and other free societies have the most progressive and risky constitutions in the history of civilization. These documents give people freedom to pursue happiness of their own choice. The problem is that if the people are not aware of the great powers that lie inside each of us, they are left susceptible to the influence of other people regarding how to acquire that happiness. The key to opening the door to all human capabilities is camouflaged with what we think will render us happy.

What makes us happy? Is it a life with no pain? Satisfied urges? Wealth? Experiencing sexual pleasure and making money will not make us happy in the way most people expect. Everyday strife, pressures, desires, and impulses cannot be avoided. We recognize happiness in contrast to unhappiness. A good example is the Eastern philosophy of yin and yang. According to the *Britannica Concise Encyclopedia*, this belief suggests that all of life consists of yin and yang, two complementary but opposite forces or principles. Yin is earth (female, passive, and dark), while yang is heaven (male, active, and light). Balance between the two creates a harmonious existence between opposite but coexisting forces. Many people try to force the yin or the yang out of the equation as a shortcut to harmony or happiness. They want dominance, not balance. This approach hasn't changed in the history of mankind;

therefore, history repeats itself. So if mankind is the solution to the earth's problems, a new awareness has to come into being to change the cycle. We must see our different cultural developments for what they are: mankind's endless pursuit of happiness (or in my simple vernacular, "feeling good").

Like other free societies, the United States has a constitution that was written to spell out rights and freedoms for human beings within a society. But does the Constitution really unlock our human potential? Does the legal guarantee of the freedom to choose one's education or employment or lifestyle actually unlock any greatness? Where is the power of freedom?

First, let's examine the definition of freedom by explaining what freedom *is not*.

- Freedom *is not* doing anything you want to do.
- Freedom *is not* "doing your thing."
- Freedom *is not* the absence of all limits and rules.

Such definitions of freedom are immature and even ignorant. At its purest level, freedom is the ability and awareness to make choices. We are all born free; the ability to choose is innate in all human beings. In a free society, our laws guarantee certain legal and cultural freedoms, but legislated freedom in itself cannot release true power. In order to extract any power from that freedom, our choices must be based on something beyond the legal definition. Many forces influence our choices, and most people are seldom aware of those influences. To access the true power of freedom, we must not allow government, religion, culture, society, environment, peer pressure, or anything else to dictate our choices.

I will lay out the details of a process any human being can follow to find the power of freedom. I will explain the actual feelings and conflicts that will occur should one choose to break free. Why bother? Isn't happiness and finding a purpose for our existence worth the effort? In addition, the power generated by true freedom can unleash the potential within all of us to solve the problems that cripple the development of humanity.

Think of the problems that exist today in our world. Our faltering economy gives evidence of flaws in the system. All social and cultural systems will show their inadequacies with time. The pursuit of a more perfect union will demand that changes take place when those flaws are exposed. It is to be expected. The societal expectation that change will happen from a posture of complacency is absurd. That complacency, which has created so many illusions in our American way of life, has to be dealt with before significant change can occur.

CHAPTER 7

SHOW ME THE POWER!

When I began my new experiment in thinking, the choices I made affected my whole environment. Friendships and other relationships changed or disappeared completely almost overnight. That was difficult, but the new direction in this social experiment, I believed, was going to be worth it. Several weeks passed before I sensed any energy coming from these new choices. The energy produced seemed to be coming from my mind. I was thinking more and differently than I had ever experienced before.

Of course, the absence of foreign substances had a chemical effect on my physical being, but there was more than that going on. The very essence of the freely made choice based on logic, rather than feelings, seemed to be the source of the energy. I was getting used to it. As in any new venture, my life change brought a certain amount of fear of the unknown and the fear of the results of these choices. One immediate result socially was the redefinition of friendship. No big surprise here!

I continued to examine the effects of the radical change I had implemented simply by making choices through logic. I did not lose my humanity or sense of feelings. I still felt compassion for my fellow human beings. The initial reaction to the lack of partying was a need for activity of a higher thrill level. Hang gliding seemed like a good solution, and I did it for three years before the risk of personal injury and also the increased site limitations made it less desirable. Besides my increased mental activity, I had much more physical energy available, and it needed an outlet. I found that a classical martial art plus an early-morning exercise routine did the trick.

I believe the effects would be specific to each individual making these changes, but the essential rewiring of mental activity would be similar. Radical changes resulting from choices made from a position of freedom separated from human emotion will immediately have the mind asking *why* and there is where a new thinking process begins. And why shouldn't it? All human beings have an ancient history of substance use. The notion that substance use in certain forms or according to proper social protocol is acceptable is absurd!

Every person has latent unique abilities and powers within that make us all *created equal*. Call it universal genius, though it appears in different forms. IQ scores and academic grades cannot measure abilities that have not yet been realized. The solutions the planet needs at this time will have to come from outside the box of conventional thinking. The phrase "We the People" from the US Constitution takes on a whole new meaning. Freedom should liberate all people to the pursuit of happiness.

It is difficult to separate my personal lifestyle changes from the change in my basic thinking patterns. I have tried to explain the changes in my thinking, which I believe are more universally pertinent. Giving up substance use, understanding and practicing sex for its logical purpose, and choosing not to use vulgar language led to the release of energy and power. Thinking more brought about more energy, more change, and more awareness of the power of true freedom. Now I want everyone to know that power.

A Goal for the United States—and Maybe the World!

Because I exist and these ideas are facts in my life and behavior, it follows *that any human being has the same power to pursue a new choice of action* through a different gateway called freedom. If not now, when? At this time in history, the need for change from within individuals couldn't be greater!

No person can argue logic using human feelings as a foundation. People have an amazing ability to confuse logic with feelings. Logic can coexist with human feelings with the increased awareness of compassion. One could argue that choices made from logic would be heartless. That is not true, because the beauty of being human is that we cannot separate emotion and logic from our nature. If all humans are created equal, how can we discard a vast majority of citizens as casualties or as useless in solving the problems pressing mankind? Of course, it is freedom of choice that may define what such citizens become, but maybe the lack of awareness of their own inherent powers is all that is missing.

Our modern society prides itself on its ability to manipulate the opinion and buying habits of the masses in one direction or another. The concept of people trying to control other people is as old as history itself. The US Constitution states the goal as "in order to form a more perfect union," a goal that did not end when the document was signed. Democratic, freedom-based governments have the ability to improve and evolve to a more perfect ideology for the greater good of society.

Overcoming Fear

The twenty-first century has so much potential for deep change in the human condition if only we can overcome our fear of change. I have already entered the early stages of a New Age of Enlightenment, and I can tell you that there is nothing to fear. Much of the world that we humans have created is an illusion. My biggest fear when my radical choices in behavior started was that such a change in my life marked the end of feeling good and being happy. I was big-time wrong. Yes, I have experienced aggravation, heartache, and failure, but that's life. Happiness, fun, and good feelings still exist and to a much greater degree.

That is why I am compelled to write this book. I feel like an explorer who just came back from an expedition of the new world, complete with road maps and surveys, and I can tell everyone, "It's okay; I've been there; it's amazing. Don't be afraid." The increased brain energy, which accelerated the thinking, didn't produce all the answers, but it made me thirsty for knowledge! This led me from zero reading to reading a book a month—biographies of significant thinkers and leaders, or books on philosophy, finance, psychology, and attitude. My quest for knowledge is never-ending. Given enough time, I believe anyone will sense the same thirst.

If you ask yourself *Why?* for long enough to get past the self-created illusions, your newfound freedom will kick in. At age fifty-eight, I cannot take for granted the amount of time I have to relate this message; therefore, I feel a sense of urgency. We need to realize that so many of the world's problems stem from substance use, but telling people to stop using because it isn't good for them doesn't work.

What I am writing isn't just about stopping substance use. That activity is just a small part of the equation of releasing the power of freedom. Decisions must be made with a total awareness of free will. That will release the power.

Academia and legal systems in themselves are not the means of mankind's evolution to a higher state of being. Look at the amazing attempt by the US government to stop the use of one particular drug called alcohol in the early twentieth century. They called it the "noble experiment," otherwise known as Prohibition. That "experiment" is proof that legislation cannot change human behavior.

I am definitely not advocating the outlawing of alcohol. This is just an observation, but isn't it amazing that a society accepts the use of alcohol and tobacco even with their proven deadly qualities? How about bars that serve alcohol to patrons who need to drive their cars home from the bar? How about the laws against drunk driving? How many patrons when leaving the bars would be able to pass the sobriety test? How much logic is being used in all this activity? What an illogical world we live in!

DISTORTED LOGIC

What passes for logic most of the time today is really rationalization; to use a more current phrase, we put a spin on a subject. People have the greatest capacity for rationalization, which is simply a way to justify our feelings. We define what is logical by the whole gamut of feelings we attach to everything we do.

We must recognize the problem of rationalization. I believe we must start with something as simple as what we ingest, whether by mouth, nose, or veins. The problem is we must be free to decide what is or is not logical in order for any power to be released, and we can't be free while under the influence of alcohol or other drugs.

The little choices made from a solely emotional basis slowly neutralize the thinking process at a core level—the level from which we would otherwise derive power. Our constitution gives us the right to choose our pursuit of happiness. In that pursuit, are we to choose insignificance or greatness? Why not greatness on a personal level?

Each human being has a definite purpose, no less or greater than another's. It is amazing to witness people coming out of whatever closet and trying to alter the perception of their behavior by the rest of the population. Their thinking involves a rich mixture of emotions to evoke compassion from the listener. Compassion is a natural response from a human being, but seeing through the illusion would aid in understanding the behavior. A nonjudgmental response with compassion is required. Until people can see beyond the self-created image of themselves, no one has the right or even the power to force a change in thinking.

The powerful inherent gift of choice makes humans truly unique. Choice makes compassion possible. If we understand that we are all equal except for the choices we make, we can have compassion for another person, because given the same circumstances, we could have been the person whose behavior we do not understand or like! We all have our own challenges.

UNDER THE INFLUENCE

My vision of the future sees a world that recognizes illogical behavior for what it is. We will look back at old film footage of people smoking cigarettes and wonder why they did that. A change in our thinking patterns will change our perceptions of our reality.

For example, we know that gravity is an undeniable natural law. Yet under the influence of LSD, we believe the illogical idea that we can jump from a building and fly! When humans accept illogical behavior, their minds build supporting ideas to rationalize one behavior on top of another. It's like an accountant trying to balance the numbers on a balance sheet that doesn't add up. The numbers have to be altered to achieve the perceived balance. The resulting balance sheet will be in error, but at a glance, it seems correct.

In the same way, flawed thinking eventually produces errors in our societies that need to be corrected. It seems we humans keep making illogical choices out of some kind of fear. We are sabotaging our own destiny toward greatness for mere pettiness. Why? With our technology, we are able to build on previous discoveries and expand our horizons. Why can't we build on what evidence we already have from history and the nature of being human and evolve to the next level?

History may show that humanity had just the right stimulus in 2010 to begin the process of internal change and alter the course of history toward a New Age of Enlightenment. Because free will must be respected, the process cannot be forced, and time will be required. Our history as a nation has been evolving for a little more than two hundred years. Are we to let all that blood and sacrifice for this grand experiment just disappear? This is one time when a vote of the majority is not needed. A few deciding in favor of change for the sake of the many can begin the revolution, not by force, but by change from within. For those who choose this, a war will sometimes be fought on the inside in order to find harmony and peace on the outside. We can build one small, logical choice upon another in order to develop the power of freedom.

What could be simpler? Yes, it is simple, but I did not say it is easy! There is always a price to be paid for greater benefit. My words give evidence that change is possible. My five-year experiment shows the dramatic effect that the freedom of the pursuit of feeling good can and does have on our development. The pleasure derived from the very easy choice of substance use is just a large smoke screen that hides the real pleasure or joy of the entirely new world just on the other side of freedom. That's where the power lies!

I have personally witnessed how we rationalize our substance use. We label alcohol and tobacco in a separate category, not considering them as drugs because they are legal. We use the word "moderation" to determine the proper use of any substance, but who determines the definition of moderation? Our society forms its own norms. Does a vote by the majority cause any illogical behavior to become logical? Why does each new generation rebel against established standards of acceptable behavior? Why doesn't the new generation change what doesn't make sense and replace it with new behavior? A barrier of fear prevents any real change. So this illusion of fear of the unknown is plaguing mankind, just as in the days of Columbus.

What happens to our youth as they come of age? Can we blame our educational systems for these rebellions and illusions? As I stated before, academia cannot be expected to respond to the needs of every human being. All the energy and enthusiasm of our

71

youth is being lost when we need it the most. The very popular saying of "say no to drugs" doesn't come close to "why not?"

A change from within in our free societies not only disarms the terrorist but also gives our youth an answer with power. The freedom to choose empowers people! Dictating law and policy only rubs people the wrong way. You cannot legislate an idea. Even with a wave of highly charged new thinkers, you can expect argument. In that argument and dialogue, new discoveries will be made. We will find solutions in our diversity.

PROS AND CONS IN AMERICA

Our economic system has created terrific wealth for those who understand its principles. Free enterprise allows anyone with a dream to pursue financial freedom. The freedom to pursue happiness is guaranteed in our Bill of Rights. Our economic system is highly developed, yet many flaws are being exposed. It is not by destroying the old system that we are going to improve it, but it does need a major tune-up. With all this wealth, why are our health-care and educational systems doing such a poor job? Why, with all the taxes, are the federal, state, and local governments running out of money to handle even the most basic functions?

Greed and arrogance run deep in our society. These issues have to be addressed on a personal level by every one of us. "We the People" need to address these issues personally if we want to continue to be free. If we allow government officials or anyone else to do our thinking for us, our civilization is lost. This cannot be allowed to happen. We are too close to our true destiny in mankind's evolution to let this happen.

Our country's arrogance or pride fuels our desire for the rest of the world to see our wealth as testimony of our superior government. When Hurricane Katrina hit us, our government wouldn't let Cuban medical teams come in and help! You can spin this any way you want, but what kind of attitude is that?

Releasing the true power of freedom will expose our arrogance as an illogical illusion. Why not take our system of government and way of life to the next level? We can develop a world where all can pursue their dreams, where everyone has effective health care available, where all can pursue knowledge to the fullest extent of their desires without going in debt.

CHANGE IS POSSIBLE

The changes I have outlined are no more impossible than our ability to change our behavior. I changed and continue to change, and so can you. Do you want to rationalize an excuse to me? Don't even try! In the last thirty years, I have been patiently growing and sometimes painfully coexisting in a society whose behavior is so absurd, I wonder if I'm not some kind of alien.

Well, I am human, no different than any other person on the planet, and it's my time to come out of the closet. My emotional development has seen me shed a lot of tears. I've come to understand that the tear shedding is a normal reaction to the emotional growth. To engage thinking and to follow through with choosing logical behavior does not nullify emotion.

I'm not suggesting we all become like Mr. Spock of *Star Trek*. We cannot separate our human nature from our emotions. The power of freedom does not only intensify brain activity; it also brings our feelings into perspective. Shedding tears effects a harmony among the tensions that caused the tears in the first place. Building one logical choice on another develops a sense of control and confidence, and confidence makes problems manageable.

Once, while sailing on a lake in California, I capsized the boat, and all of us on board landed in the water. A few panicked, but I found myself encouraging everyone to stay calm and get back in the boat. The incident was a very minor one, but my calm demeanor was automatic.

When we block our own access to the elevated powers of the mind with the mindless pursuit of pleasure, we shouldn't be surprised at the stresses and problems we create for ourselves. Look at all the advertising dollars spent on prescription drugs. Given our present economic system, do you think there are industries that don't want us to change our habits? The use of alternate sources of propulsion and energy and the decreased use of drugs, tobacco, and alcohol would change the cash flow of many unscrupulous companies. They represent only a fraction of the self-interested groups that want to influence our behavior. The easiest way to manipulate the masses is not to let them think and to keep them medicated in one form or another.

We forfeit much of our freedom of choice to forces we don't even recognize. What are these forces? Advertising, political rhetoric, and even religion, to name a few. The result is a creation of a world of illusions that we foolishly believe to be security. We use so little of our imagination and potential because of fear. Take, for example, the automobile. When cars were first mass-produced, they were heavy and consumed a lot of gasoline. We developed lighter construction materials and electronic fuel-injection systems, but we still didn't see the bigger picture.

These fuel-efficient solutions, though effective against the immediate problem, just postponed the real problems of pollution and energy consumption. Do the automotive industry and oil-affiliated businesses want us to discover alternate means of transportation? No; their own small thinking, fear, and greed have blurred their vision.

RECOGNIZING BARRIERS

The true power of freedom can liberate our thinking, so greed and small-box thinking can be diminished or eliminated completely. We build our lives around hypotheses that allow illogical behavior, and when issues arise—whether physical, mental, or societal—we try to find solutions within that very small box of thinking that we created. We rationalize assumptions that may be entirely false. There was a time when people assumed the world was flat, so they accepted all sorts of assumed facts arising from that hypothesis.

Another example is bipolar disorder. This phenomenon is well-documented by far greater minds than mine. Many medications are available to treat the disorder. But what if the disorder is self-created through personal use of mood-altering substances in the first place? If a person uses mood-altering substances to the extent of creating a mental disorder, is prescribing other substances really an effective solution?

What about the socially accepted practice of entertaining corporate clients with alcohol? What is the purpose? Is it to relax their thinking capabilities and influence them more easily? See just how deeply ingrained accepted habits have become without anyone ever asking the question *Why*? Likewise, the real question about sexual activity of any kind is not a matter of freedom of choice of partners or techniques, or right or wrong, but *why*! The simple rationalization that "it feels good" or "I'm in love" is primitive at the very least. (If you think I am anti-sex, please refer to the five-year experiment. I know sex feels good, but that's not a logical reason for the activity.) Our sexual being can no more be removed from our nature than the rest of our emotional makeup.

All of us have internal energies that need to be diverted through the power of freedom, so we can evolve to a greater destiny. Mankind has been trying to evolve, as history has shown us. Technology has evolved at a much greater rate than our human potential. We are much more valuable in our essence than any technology that we have developed through the centuries.

It is time, now, to use all the newly discovered freedoms that have always existed to fulfill the true destiny of humankind. We need to re-create ourselves to better understand the need and function of government and religion in our lives. Until we begin that process, government and religion will reflect very biased interpretations of reality. Killing people in the name of a particular system of government or religion is an extreme example of illogical behavior promoted by organized institutions.

It is our social nature to associate with like-minded people and form friendships. During the five-year experiment, my friends were people who shared substance use with me. When my choices led me in another direction, these friends disappeared. My reasoning here is that like-minded groups of any kind can organize to form a stronger influential opinion. Even a group whose numbers are mathematically a very small portion of the society as a whole can have an influence. A new idea, such as the one I am introducing, with effective media, could start such a group. A group of superthinkers could in fact become a beacon of light to the maze of illogical behavior that our civilization practices. At least exposing biased thinking from a new perspective may help us find solutions to the planet's challenges.

The very freedom that permits illogical behavior can never be removed, nor should it. Otherwise the power of freedom can also never be realized. Returning the power to the people from whom it originated in the first place would be a grand goal at first. The realization of each individual's importance and value in a society would make for a powerful group of like-minded people.

If the United States became a beacon for the rest of the planet, broadcasting what freedom can really become, our influence would be effective. When our freedom became the source of solutions to our problems, the world would begin to realize the true essence of the power of freedom. Sometimes results are the only facts that can be believed. How much courage we can really muster at this time of urgency has yet to be realized.

I dream of the day when the power of freedom is released in our society—when we will witness solutions and ideas coming from people whom our society doesn't know exist! As these people become aware of *thinking* for the first time in their lives, they will develop power and significance. We will discover new ideas and solutions where none existed before! That is a dream worth fighting for and dying for. As I mentioned before, I have visited many cemeteries and always notice the birth and death dates on the tombstones. I am intrigued by what happened in the time represented by the dash— the life between the dates. What we achieve is not as important as what we become in our short journey.

CHAPTER 8

HISTORY AND CHANGE

Any study in History 101 will show evidence of prior great civilizations, such as the Greeks, the Romans, the Egyptians, the Mayans, and the Aztecs. In every case, the system eventually broke down and failed to evolve further. Why?

No system of government could ever achieve perfection, of course, but somewhere in those systems there must have been a ceiling past which those societies could evolve no further. The breakdown came from within. Why can't we learn from this?

Our system of government is the most evolved in the history of mankind. It has the ability to change! That ability is a vital ingredient. Our ability to improve our government opens a limitless horizon to a fertile environment in which the human species can transgress its self-imposed limitations and develop into something more. We must not rationalize that family genetics, environment, or social conditions make such change impossible. If I could make the changes, there are no excuses for anyone else!

The gravest threat to our society today is its interpretation of the "pursuit of happiness." A freedom-based society must allow freedom of choice. We cannot legislate the freedom of choice, but we can educate all the people about the power of true freedom.

Of course, it will require thinking outside of the box. Our modern systems of freedom-based governments have the means to think outside of the box, which is why they have the potential for greatness. With the challenges facing the planet today, we need to learn from the past and to imagine a new future unlike anything in history—a New Age of Enlightenment. This new vision can inspire a much-needed emotional response—one strong enough to break us away from the social disease called complacency!

Unfortunately, due to our emotional makeup, we usually won't change our behavior or actions without strong emotional stimuli, despite what our intellect is telling us. Education alone isn't enough. The highest form of leadership or influence is necessary. Look at what Gandhi was able to accomplish in a relatively short time! India earned freedom through blood and sacrifice. Freedom at any level always comes at a price. Freedom given doesn't carry the same value. Freedom of choice is only a doorway to releasing great power.

Finding solutions to our worldwide problems will require the participation of all the inhabitants of the planet. Freedom-based governments are not the only societies out there. Some of the illusions we portray to the rest of the world through the media are highly materialistic, wrongly suggesting that consumption in itself will produce happiness.

Other societies may not believe or respect that ideology. This friction can hinder the exchange of ideas with these other societies. Influential leadership is the only answer to this dilemma. Free societies have to earn that influence through change from within. Simply stated, if we are a great society, we must show it. Societies need effectual, influential leadership to direct the improvement of their standard of living. Freedom of choice allows the thinking citizen to accept that leadership. This relationship between a society and its leader forms powerful synergy for the advancement of a civilization.

If individuals and their leaders are to solve problems, we must remember that solutions will come from individuals with the freedom to choose. No one can be left out of the equation. Within society, all are needed to maintain inner harmony. When people must make difficult choices, they may need a helping hand. Most importantly, everyone must be told of the power that each individual possesses. If a few people hoard this knowledge about the power of freedom, we will see blatant disrespect for humankind and terrible crimes against society.

GAINING RESPECT

At no other time in history has the whole planet faced so many common challenges. The common denominator facing everyone is our need to find a way to survive, not just improve our quality of life! The current economic problems will affect vast numbers of people in their ability to feed and shelter themselves. The world is looking for solutions on a global level. The Internet and other forms of communication have drawn us closer as a global community.

Among non-freedom-based societies today, respect for the United States is very low. Many even fear us—perhaps with good reason, since we were the first to use the atomic bomb in war (against civilians, no less). I am not judging the decision, but the bomb's use is evidence that a free society is capable of committing the most violent of acts against humanity to gain victory. Amazingly enough, this action took place while we were fighting a people ready to commit suicide in order to prevent our victory. This behavior is alien to our culture. My ex-father-in-law was an officer aboard a naval ship under attack by kamikazes. Judging from his account, an enemy who looks at death as a way to heaven is a frightening foe, and this type of enemy shows amazing similarities to our present-day terrorists.

How do you nuke an opposing idea? You don't. The best way to defeat an idea is with another idea! Sharing the true power of freedom with the rest of the world could bring a new respect for the free world. The misinterpreted image of freedom in these other cultures is precisely what gives them the energy to want to destroy us. The only way to gain their respect on the ideological level is to show them what the true power of freedom can accomplish when it is released.

Cultures that are alien to us or even hostile toward us still have knowledge and wisdom to share with the rest of humanity. Unless the freedom-based societies advance to a higher level of awareness and gain the respect of these other societies, there is little chance that the inhabitants of this planet will come together to solve its problems. Leadership through the highest level of influence is the only way the rest of the planet will become convinced of another idea.

We have to respect that other cultures need freedom of choice. We can't force people to be free or to respect each other or us. Compassion and intellect must work in harmony. Perfection is impossible, but improvement isn't!

Don't Forget the Individual!

All this talk of societies is taking away the vital importance of the individual. All people have a great importance and purpose, and their choices matter to all of us. But first that awareness must be made known, and that is where my burning desire to write comes from. I believe that change is possible and that the historic timing may be right.

Where do all of my ideas come from? It certainly is not from years of conventional academia! The small choices I made starting thirty-five years ago created energy and a thinking machine. My increased reading and observations constantly added data to my consciousness. My purpose and importance are no more special than the purpose and importance of any other person on the planet. The same energy will have a different effect on each individual. Each person's road map to his or her purpose is unraveled from within.

At this time in history, it is amazing how the need for change makes itself so evident! If change does not occur, the very continuation of our democratic and free societies is at stake. Freedom needs to go to the next level, so we can continue to exist. If not, than this two-hundred-year-old experiment will disappear!

Freedom was never meant to eliminate the tensions involved in the choices we make. Choices made for only freedom's sake will always lean toward the path of least resistance, and that default state is the hidden threat to our existence. The historic inauguration of President Obama shows to the world that in the United States, freedom and democracy can stand up to the scrutiny of its own constitution.

The social and environmental stage is set for change, but we must recognize the need for individuals to change. Obama and his leadership team cannot solve the challenges that face America. Study the history of the birth and growth of the United States. The founding fathers of the Constitution not only had tremendous courage and strength of character, but also the genius required to create the foundation of a more perfect system of government. Through much pain and sacrifice, that system continues to evolve.

FIGHT BOREDOM

For a society to thrive, it needs a vision for the future. This vision can inspire a greater purpose for its existence. These days, whatever free time we manage to etch out seems to be filled with mindless activities like TV, video games and listening to our iPods. I am not judging these activities, but they do provide fertile ground for complacency and boredom. Boredom was one of the hurdles that I encountered early in my changing. Boredom is different from complacency but just as dangerous. I replaced boredom with exciting activities like hang gliding, catamaran racing on heavy seas, and skydiving. It works for me! I do not believe it is possible to stop substance use without replacing it with some other activity. We all need a vision for the future and a greater purpose for our existence.

Boredom is human nature's way of letting us know that something is missing; all that greatness and potential in each human being is trying to make itself evident. What makes this notion so confusing for substance users is that boredom is camouflaged through illusion, so the doorway to the solution of boredom is lost.

Let me put it another way. We have to sense boredom in order to find a pathway out to excitement. Excitement is the release of *energy*, which is the true power of freedom. When we are having fun and feeling good, the thought of trading that in for boredom is frightening. I have been there, and the truth is just on the other side of boredom. Freedom of choice is the liberator. Facing boredom and complacency squarely is the only way out.

Again, the new choices we make will create an immediate sensation of tension or frustration, but the doorway is just past that. It is as if some kind of force is trying to keep mankind from realizing its potential. Now we see the true enemy for what it is: a lie and an illusion.

If anyone had the notion that the world was flat, Christopher Columbus's successful voyage forced a change in thinking, and what became of that argument?

Columbus could say, "I have made the journey!" He had the proof of personal experience.

The discoveries I made on my journey are no different from those that could be made by anyone else. The difference is that I went to the abyss, made some observations, and returned with a new awareness. We have always had substances available to us. The use and discovery of more substances doesn't make us a more advanced civilization. Why do I keep coming back to substance use? My exposure during the sixties and seventies made me see how prevalent substance use was becoming in every facet of society. It is a major catalyst in the development of much of the illogical behavior of the human species.

WAKE UP!

Exposing the illusion that is cast on human potential has never been more important. The system of freedom that exists in our society today has never before seen such a threat to its survival! The challenges that we face today could extinguish the flame that was lit more than two hundred years ago. The Boy Scout motto, "be prepared," could be applied here, except we are not prepared for these multifaceted problems hitting all at the same time.

Consider an analogy of what happens when the country needs more military personnel for national defense. Boot camp becomes a wake-up call for each soldier to move into the ready-to-fight mode. Someone has to get in the soldier's face and scream, "Wake up!"

Maybe that is the purpose for my existence at this time in history. My understanding of human nature tells me that screaming in someone's face may not be the most effective method, especially for a choice that requires free will, but I need to get everyone's attention somehow.

Do we really value our freedom enough to sacrifice our comfortable complacency? We can learn a lot from that period in our history when the African Americans were slaves in the South. Some wanted freedom bad enough to risk all and escape through the Underground Railroad. What about the slaves who traded freedom for the security of a slave's lifestyle? Are we to let fear of the unknown or our own complacency rob us of our potential? We have the potential to form a more perfect union and transgress our present limitations!

The US Constitution's principles are the foundation of our government—a government by and for the people, with freedom granted to every citizen. Our government has been trying to perfect these foundational ideals since its conception. If "We the People" continue to reinterpret the words of the Constitution with emotionally confused thinking, our way of life will not be sustainable by future generations.

As it becomes more difficult to explain our society's behavior to our children, an even greater fog of illusion hinders future generations. This could be a mechanism for self-destruction that is creeping up right behind us. If we miss this historic timing for change from within now, this time in history will be seen as the beginning of the end of our way of life and government.

That belief is why I cannot stand idly by and do nothing! This illogical behavior's march toward self-destruction can't be tolerated; it is time to act! For thirty-five years, I have been waiting for the right time for my words. I have been training myself for this time in history since I was born.

Do my words bother you? If so, you are probably thinking from within a very small box you created a long time ago, and you are not even aware of it. I exist; therefore, another option is possible!

Back to Basic Principles

When our country was just starting out, I am sure that European countries were wondering what we, as a new nation, would do with our freedom. A country governed by the people was a risky proposition at best. The monarchies at the time, I'm sure, did not believe that people could rule themselves. Submission to a sovereign king was considered the only way a people could coexist in a civilized, orderly manner. In essence, other nations feared a free society, because they thought the result would be a nation of people whose emotions ran too rampant to allow them to rule themselves effectively.

It is no great revelation that human emotions are capable of great distortion of logic. Greed and pride can have a negative impact on a group of people forming a civilized, free government. Freedom, when given to people lacking in disciplined character, can produce chaos. Basically, other forms of government force such discipline of character by simply removing as much freedom of choice as possible. This produces an environment that essentially blocks access to the power of freedom.

When our forefathers authored the Constitution, they implied that a deity was overseeing all of our behavior, providing an unwritten moral code as a basis for all of our laws. It was the only way our forefathers could understand how our negative emotions could be controlled within a free society. Today we interpret freedom as our constitutional right to fulfill any feelings we have in the pursuit of happiness. It is almost as if we believe that by removing the deity from the Constitution, we can form a more perfect union.

As I mentioned earlier, we need to be free of any organized religion that tries to eliminate our freedom of choice, but this should not to be misinterpreted to mean religion does not serve a vital role in society.

Our dazed obsession with pursuing freedom for freedom's sake has obscured the doorway to the true power of freedom and has produced much of the absurdity that we are witnessing today. In our quest, we have lost the meaning of responsibility, accountability, and commitment. These are the unwritten virtues of our human potential that keep our system of government functioning.

The Constitution was well thought out by people who put their lives in jeopardy and placed checks and balances in the words to guarantee the longevity of this new country. The document was to establish the foundation of freedom in this new government. All men are created equal! The word "men" was meant to mean people of any sex, color, or creed, but the thinking at the time needed to evolve to understand this idea.

Today our society's thinking has evolved, but until we realize the true power of freedom, the interpretation of "pursuit of happiness" can still be used to validate all kinds of illogical behavior. We cannot pursue a more perfect union and happiness unless we also aim for a higher level of ethics. The Constitution has a system of checks and balances included so that no single branch of the government can overpower the others. The judicial system is the only branch that lacks this balancing fail-safe.

What system do we have to balance our emotional behavior? We as individuals have a system called discipline!

Change must come first from within before we can change outward behavior. Now more than ever, flaws in our systems are being exposed. These systems include personal lifestyles and governmental or corporate-management ethics. The financial fiascoes we are witnessing today are an indication of a much greater malaise that exists in our society. Spending more than we make is both a personal and governmental issue.

I am challenged just as much as the next person on this issue. Where did we start losing the save-for-a-rainy-day concept? Our politicians, unfortunately, reflect our society's flaws in financial management. What's worse is that they spend money that isn't theirs! Whatever happened to a balanced budget that allocated money that was already available?

All these problems stem from changes that have taken place since the sixties. This change is reversible! My words can only help illuminate other minds with solutions to these and all the other challenges we are facing today. Our interpretation of freedom has gradually been neutralizing the energy that could have been released in past years.

ONLY IN THE MOVIES?

There was a movie recently released that became almost a cult phenomenon among teenage girls. It was called *Twilight*. It was pegged as an epic romance, and I was intrigued to watch when it became available on TV. What I found remarkable was the kind of romance it depicted. It displayed emotional intensity without physical intimacy. Even though the story was about a vampire and a human, it showed a male who, despite great physical desire, restrained himself from physical contact with the girl he loved. He demonstrated self-control for a greater purpose. Yes, it's a vampire movie, but it shows that this kind of relationship between the sexes can exist, I believe, and that was what intrigued the adolescent girls.

"It's only a movie," you say. Is it possible for humans to practice self-control and other logical behavior for the greater good? What we choose as entertainment sometimes gives evidence of what is going on in the mind. The new generation coming of age today is facing a world of contradictions and illusions. Young people are asking questions. Sexual education today has to explain this biological function of human bodies in a much more enlightened way for it to make sense to these new minds just becoming aware.

The whole approach of explaining human sexuality in terms of sexual preference and personal desire for pleasure does not answer the most important questions. Telling young people to have "safe sex" and enjoy themselves does not solve problems.

I see hope in the movie *Twilight*, because it suggests that a person can choose, logically, to control his sexual desire. A generation born into nonsense can somehow see clearly the true power of freedom. A revolution from within could happen, just as it did once before in our country.

Can you imagine for a moment the feelings the first Pilgrims had when they landed in the New World? They were full of hope and wonder at the new world of opportunity. How about the immigrants who landed at Ellis Island in the last hundred years, full of wonder and anticipation for the opportunities of freedom in a new land? They treasured freedom of choice and the opportunity to make something of their lives that they couldn't have in the old country. Do "We the People" treasure our freedom? Have we become so complacent that we need to redefine freedom by rationalizing absurdity and illogical behavior in our interpretation of the Constitution? Maybe new immigrants found happiness in the mere opportunity to chase their dreams, instead of trying to redefine freedom as a right of entitlement to any pleasure we desire.

With all the technology and capabilities we have available for instant gratification, maybe we have lost sight of what really renders human happiness. President John Kennedy stated, "Ask not what your country can do for you; ask what you can do for your country." Maybe we should be asking what we can do for each other. When we engage in freedom as a pursuit of self-gratification, how can we even be aware of the needs of other human beings all around us?

ARROGANCE AND GREED

In a recent visit to the new Gettysburg National Military Park, my spirit was stirred from deep within. I found myself standing in the visitor's center, shedding tears at the price our nation paid to stay united as one nation. Many conflicting ideologies of the South and North were brought to a head, and a new meaning of freedom was born. Amazingly enough, both sides had huge issues with the evolution of the concept of freedom that was originally introduced in our Constitution. Can you imagine if a huge portion of the economy was based on free slave labor? It made for a huge profit margin and an obvious disparity in the distribution of wealth. If you strain all the tension out of ideological differences, you find greed and arrogance at the center.

We are no different today! People who profit from existing systems and their inherent faults do not want change. Unfortunately, they are caught up in small thinking. Still today, labor costs make up the largest part of the budget of any business. Can there be any question as to why companies are moving operations to other countries? It is the nature of business to strive for a large profit margin.

The future of freedom and wealth distribution isn't in communism or socialism but rather in people being recognized as equals from their conception and economic systems being developed on the foundation of mutual benefit. Generous profit margins can still be obtained with a highly motivated workforce in place to share mutual interest.

Does this sound impossible? Not if you think outside of the box. I have found success in applying some of these concepts in systemizing a simple contracting and painting business. You have to reach beyond the fear of keeping the masses of people financially ignorant and unaware. Could you imagine the alcohol and tobacco industries seeing dramatic decreases in the use of their products? What kind of lobbying and advertising campaign would they launch? To what lengths would they go to stop the decline?

Can you imagine minds that have been in hibernation suddenly changing their thinking patterns and becoming enlightened with a new vision? I can! The power of freedom is screaming to be released after centuries of being captive behind all kinds of illusions. "We the People" are still responsible for the systems that exist today! We allow businesses and politicians to manipulate our thinking for their benefit. Greed and arrogance exist in all of us. Can you blame businesses from profiting from our ignorance and stupidity?

The true power of freedom exploding onto the whole scene can awaken a New Age of Enlightenment. Just as in the time of the Civil War, a new meaning of "freedom" needs to be introduced into the public consciousness. Striving for a more perfect union doesn't mean an absence of mistakes. We cannot be naive enough to think that greed and arrogance will disappear. However, releasing the power of freedom will shine a very bright light on the faults and foolishness that exist in our society. As long as we can see through the illusions and fog, we can change long-existing patterns of thinking to create a new world.

CHAPTER 9

A New Perspective

Releasing the power of freedom will cause our society to evolve in every area, including the economy. Wealth should move freely to every human being in proportion to the work contributed to society. However, free enterprise without compassion leaves room for another human emotion called greed. Rich Devos in his book *Compassionate Capitalism* lays out a very effective means for capitalism to work harmoniously with both intellect and emotion.

My purpose in writing is not to give solutions to the world's problems. For that I am not qualified. My purpose is to raise awareness and expose a doorway to a new source of human energy that is both intellectual and emotional. The energy has always existed, just like gunpowder, electricity, and atomic energy. But this source of energy within all human beings has a vastly greater potential to change the planet and find the most elusive solutions to the world's problems.

How do I get this message across? I cannot do it alone, but I hope that writing this book is a start. I expect this writing will cause a lot of controversy, and I accept that. These ideas contradict centuries of human conditioning, perhaps even on a genetic level. We cannot escape the physical history of our genetic composition, which may have been affected by the substances our ancestors used.

UNPREPARED

I do not believe that the challenges facing us today were clearly visible thirty years ago. Most of us expected that threats to our society would come from outside our borders. Politicians constantly sold the buildup of defense systems against foreign threats, both physical and ideological.

Consequently, our current society is not prepared for the challenges we face from within. Statistics from our educational system testify that the vast majority of graduates lack basic skills of reading, writing, and arithmetic. Can we expect solutions to our vast economic problems when most young people barely grasp the elementary principles of economics? I don't think so.

The solution is simple but not easy: unleash the true power of freedom and awaken all that genius that lays dormant in all those citizens of the United States and the rest of the planet! Yes, change is scary, but the alternative is worse. Consider this analogy. A man who has just lost his job goes to a bar to talk and drink with his friends. How many solutions will come out of all those conversations and the investment of his time and energy? By rewiring our thinking patterns and changing knee-jerk habits, we can begin to deal with real problems facing us today.

President Obama's inauguration ceremony and the parties that celebrated it showed plenty of emotion. We humans easily get fired up and then turn around and rationalize having a big party and getting wasted! Having a big party is a rational response to emotional excitement, but the use of substances for whatever reason is illogical. We have great difficulty separating *emotional reactions* from *logical thinking.*

"All You Need Is Love"

The old Beatles song "All You Need Is Love" suggests something about the necessity and the confusion concerning love, the greatest of human characteristics. The definition of "love" has been mixed so heavily with emotion that its meaning is clouded. The feeling of love creates an unstable state of being that often has been used to rationalize behavior.

But love is more than an emotion. It is a choice made by free will. Choosing to love, with or without the attached feelings, is far more enduring and stable.

I am not saying that our emotions are good or bad, but they are an undeniable part of our human nature. We don't want to deny our emotions. Yet we often deny the logical *thinking* part of our minds to rationalize illogical behavior and block our greater potential as human beings. You can be the judge as to what actions constitute a sin against the nature of mankind! Is denying our minds the process of thinking any more natural than denying our feelings?

My own experience testifies to the development of greater compassion that occurs when the mind is not left dormant in our pursuit of happiness. We are so similar to one another that it should be impossible for any of us to judge another's behavior. Even our pursuit of a more perfect union in government needs to involve people who engage thinking on a higher level and think outside of the box. We will need to continue to have laws for a long time to come, and those laws must protect the survival and quality of our physical and environmental world. Our *thinking* must rise above the present fluff of petty ideas.

"We the People"

More than ever before in history, we need to harness the awesome resources implied in the phrase "We the People." During World War II, we mobilized to run the factories and support the military. We were still in the old industrial economy. Our economies have now evolved to an age of technology and information exchange. The new-world economies need ideas that do not yet exist or that can be viewed from a new perspective.

Academia is only scratching the surface of development and extraction of new ideas. Our schools need to evolve to a higher level in order to be effective for a greater number of students. That evolution will occur automatically when the need arises, and that will be when the so-called common person begins to change from within. We as a species can no longer waste all the resources that already exist in every single individual. Why does our society rely only on the relative few who participate in and flourish in our educational systems for solutions to our problems? Could it be that vast numbers of the population are in a self-induced dormant state of existence, waiting to be awakened? I believe this to be the case.

START RIGHT HERE!

The same old behavior is not going to change the future. The uniqueness of the United States of America relative to the rest of the free world is its diversity of people. We have representatives from every race and culture. This is the very reason that the revolution of thinking should start here in the United States. As a nation, we could truly be a beacon of light for the rest of the world. People throughout the world could relate with the people of the United States. If change is possible here, change is possible anywhere!

There is no question that the rest of the planet is watching the United States to see how the people and their government will respond to the extreme challenges that exist today. The world stage is set! A revolution of change from within would expose the absurdity of terrorist activity. Their rhetoric would dissipate into nonsense.

Two Inspiring Examples

Dr. Ben Carson's book *Gifted Hands* is one of the books I have read on my personal journey. To witness in words the excitement of one man's journey in a specific science and see discoveries of new knowledge and new questions is inspiring to me. This man knows from experience the marvels of the human brain. Dr. Carson could make a strong argument for caring for our own brains, but we humans do not want anyone slowing down our feel-good pursuit of happiness—just look how seriously we take the warnings on cigarette labels!

Deep within our brains, there is a calling to greatness, to a higher level of existence, yet we humans keep blocking that impulse because of our petty idea that freedom to pursue happiness will bring us to some kind of self-made greatness. We have created small-box thinking for ourselves, and it keeps us trapped. If this folly continues, we deserve the nightmare that we will create. I cannot believe that. We have come so far in technology and our basic structure of civilization. We are at a threshold that is pleading for us to enter, if we are only brave enough to step through the doorway.

Just recently, I was also greatly inspired by a man who, by his own creative thinking process, started a new business and created many jobs. He saw the need for an environmentally friendly cooling device and looked at the problem from a new perspective. He simply applied solar energy to a fan in order to cool attic space. He also saw the need to keep the production materials and labor in the continental United States. His individual effort counteracted some of the job losses in our current economic crisis. His ingenuity is an example of the hidden wonders that lie dormant in each of us.

There are those who think mankind has limited resources on this planet. The unleashing of the true power of freedom would make that statement irrelevant. With all the means of transportation we have today at our disposal, doesn't it seem odd that most of the technology responsible was invented thousands of years ago, and all we have done is improve upon it? The invention of the wheel and the combustion engine took transportation to where it is today. Thinking within that narrow paradigm has led us to pollution and the need for oil.

Greed is a human emotion that has kept us stagnant for years. That emotion has also made many complacent against change. Industries that exist and function for profit in spite of the consequences exist because of greed. Releasing the power of freedom will enable us to discover new energy and a new means of transportation that is in harmony with our environment.

What kind of government programs can solve our problems? President Obama's town meetings are showing blatant evidence that people are looking to him to save them from themselves. Can we expect one man or government to find all the solutions to our current challenges? No, we cannot! Energy and power from our greatest resource, the human mind, is right there in front of us. All that is needed is a new idea to blow away the fog blinding our perspective.

Exposing new hidden human potential would be enough to start a revolution of *thinking*! Once a mind is introduced to a new idea or perspective, it is altered forever. It may take some time for the metamorphosis to take place, but change is inevitable.

My vision of a New Age of Enlightenment is a world without substance use—a world where sexual activity is respected while "We The People" work together for the betterment of mankind. In this new world, everyone is respected as unique and equal. New advances in technology break barriers with ideas that were never dreamed of before. The true genius of every human being is realized. Is that optimistic enough for you? A magnificent new world is just waiting to become real beyond the illusions of today.

CHAPTER 10

Entering a New Age of Enlightenment

The old slogan of the sixties, "Sex, drugs, and rock and roll," had a significant impact on the changing times, and the results just fifty years later are staggering: financial and corporate institutions failing, educational systems failing, health-care systems failing—impressive results! Yet there exists at the core of our nation the potential to reverse errors in thinking and start a new revolution from within, the likes of which have never been seen before in history.

The most difficult question we have as a nation is how to deal with failure in our pursuit of a more perfect union. Giving up is not the solution. I can only speak in terms of personal failure and guilt that I have had to accept in my own transformation. The change in direction that took place thirty-five years ago did not produce a perfect being; on the contrary, I still deal with failure and guilt.

How can we as a nation deal with our failures and move on to greater freedom and a better world? We must follow the same pattern that an individual follows when dealing with failure and guilt.

EMOTION, LOGIC, SPIRIT

In order to access the power within ourselves, we must first recognize and balance the three aspects that make us uniquely human: emotion, logic, and spirit. While we can never achieve a life built solely on logic, we must learn to *think*, to move beyond making a choice based solely on emotion. The structure for achieving balance between emotion and logic is rooted in the spiritual.

I realize the subject of spirituality is deeply personal, and I will not impose my belief on anyone. Each individual must identify the parameters of a belief structure that supports his or her pursuit of a higher state of being. For starters, a belief system or faith must acknowledge that we humans have great dignity and limitless inert potential within. Each of us has a defined purpose, a reason to exist.

At the heart of spirituality is free will. No government or religion or institution can dictate to the individual. Freedom is not the right to do anything you please. It is not the right to feel good, emotionally or physically, without regard to logic or consideration of potential consequences to others. Freedom is the right to think, to choose logically, and to use the energy created from thought to benefit others.

EVERYONE FAILS

Second, to overcome failure and move on to victory and accomplishment, we must learn that it is okay to fail. Everyone fails at one time or another. Every failure is a step toward success, because we learn what *not* to do! We examine the failure and start again. Every choice we make either creates energy-transforming power or blocks its development by simultaneously creating an illusion. When we exist in that illusion, all theories and assumptions are like sand castles on a beach and will not last.

Our laws and constitution can only serve as a basic guideline to our code of behavior. One of the greatest dangers our society faces today is amending our constitution with illogically formulated assumptions. Trying to bend logic with our self-created illusions could seriously undermine the rock-solid foundation our forefathers forged with much sacrifice and difficulty.

FIND YOUR ROAD MAP

Third, we must realize that every person has a built-in road map that leads to his or her purpose. You cannot recognize that purpose until you let go of self-made illusions, especially those created by substance use and feel-good, knee-jerk reactions. I remember well all the illusions I created for myself when I started the five-year experiment. Those illusions nearly blocked my way out of the experiment. The only success I found was in the power of freedom I accessed by making choices contrary to what my feelings or emotions were pressuring me to do. I found another reality—a logical, workable reality—just beyond the nonsense.

When I think of how many scientists are trying to unravel the mysteries of the universe, I am astonished. They have not even begun to understand the greatest secrets and marvels in the human mind. The simplest decisions, born of free will, can create an energy that I call the power of freedom. This energy starts a chain reaction in the mind so near and accessible to everyone. We are all born equal!

How we perceive each other has a lot to do with the illusions we have created in our minds. If we eliminate the illusions, the substances, the fear of thinking, the dependence on emotion—in other words, if we choose true freedom and use the energy it creates—we will each find purpose and success that can transcend the individual and transform our nation and the world.

Without the initial freedom of choice, no power can be realized. It is an act of the will! You do not casually stumble upon it. Any free human being can release this power from within. This freedom does not discriminate! When we individually and collectively harness the power of freedom and choice, we can solve our problems and create a New Age of Enlightenment where poverty doesn't exist, where greater harmony exists among cultures, where everyone realizes opportunity and purpose in existence.

Can a high-school graduate and housepainter be so different from any other inhabitant of the planet? If I can change, anyone can change. And if everyone can and will change, the world will change.

My challenge to the citizens of the free world and the rest of the planet is this:

WHAT ARE YOU WAITING FOR?